Plagues
and Politics

Fitzhugh Mullan, M.D.

Plagues
and Politics

The Story of the United States
Public Health Service

Basic Books, Inc., Publishers   New York

*This book is dedicated to the
men and women of the
United States Public Health Service
who have provided scientific knowledge
and clinical skill to the
American nation and the world
for almost two centuries.*

Copyright © 1989 by Basic Books, Inc.
Printed in the United States of America
Produced by David H. Roland
Designed by Charles O. Hyman
89 90 91 92 RRD 9 8 7 6 5 4 3 2 1

Library of Congress CIP Data

Mullan, Fitzhugh.
   Plagues and politics: the story of the United States Public
Health Service/Fitzhugh Mullan.
      p.   cm.
   Bibliography: p. 218
   Includes index.
   ISBN 0–465–05779–9
   1. United States. Public Health Service—History. I. Title.
[DNLM: 1. United States. Public Health Service. 2.
National Health Program—history—United States. 3. Public
Health—history—United States. WA 11 AA1 M9p]
RA445.M75 1989
353.0084'1—dc20
DNLM/DLC
for Library of Congress   89–42517
                                                              CIP

Contents

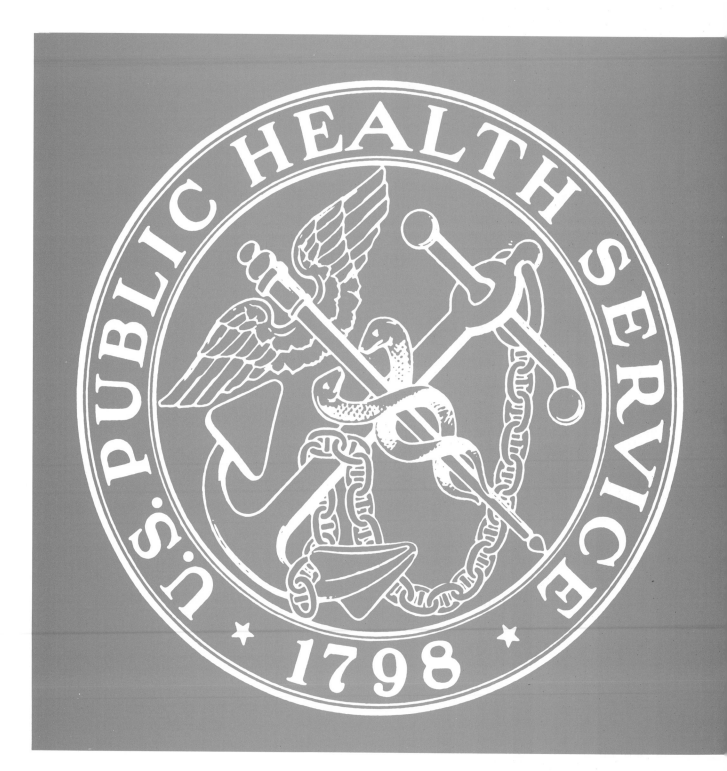

Foreword

In 1900, Surgeon General Walter Wyman undoubtedly knew all of the 107 commissioned officers on duty at the time and many of the 985 civilian employees that comprised the United States Public Health Service (then called the Marine Hospital Service). When I became Surgeon General in 1981, that was not possible. The PHS had 7,100 commissioned officers and more than 45,000 civil service employees. The agencies of the PHS were engaged in clinical care, disease surveillance, and biomedical research throughout the country and the world. Scientists at the National Institutes of Health, for instance, were working at the frontier of genetic engineering. Epidemiologists from the Centers for Disease Control working with the World Health Organization had just completed their epochal achievement eradicating smallpox. The physicians and nurses of the Indian Health Service were well on their way to the goal of reducing the rate of Indian infant mortality below that of the nation as a whole. The PHS was an enormously exciting place to work but it was barely possible to comprehend—let alone know—the varied programs and people of the modern Public Health Service.

That is why the Centennial year of the Commissioned Corps, 1989, has proved timely and important for the Public Health Service. It has given us reason to pause and reflect on our roots and our mission. What are our triumphs and where have we come up short? What does our history tell us about the past and—importantly—the future of public health in America? In anticipation of the Centennial and in this reflective spirit, I asked Dr. Fitzhugh Mullan to research and write the history of the Public Health Service. I did this so that the fascinating story would be available not only to members of the PHS but to the public at large and, especially, to young people considering careers in the health sciences. *Plagues and Politics* is that story.

My reading of *Plagues and Politics*, borne out by my eight years as Surgeon General, is that public health in America is a work in progress. That, indeed, is as it should be since the PHS is a product of the ever-changing scientific capabilities and political tendencies of the American nation. That means, though, that the agenda of the PHS is always unfinished, its programs always in transition. On the occasion of the Centennial and the publication of *Plagues and Politics*, I would like to offer some of my thoughts on the future of the PHS and public health in America.

First, the PHS has been at the forefront of the nation's struggle against tobacco (nicotine) addiction since Surgeon General Luther Terry released his historic report on smoking a quarter of a century ago. Under his leadership and that of his successors, we have made significant progress in combatting the health impact of smoking in the United States. Based upon those accomplishments and in spite of the powerful economic forces promoting the use of tobacco, I can foresee a smoke-free America. The PHS, though, must remain vigilant in its leadership of this campaign, continuing to provide the science base and the public forum crucial to the national movement that involves the entire fabric of our country — private as well as public; schools, churches, and legislatures; employers, celebrities, and the person on the street. Our future success depends on the PHS and the health community reaching those groups where an important difference can be made—children and adolescents, women, minorities, and blue-collar workers. The life, health, and longevity of many of us alive today, as well as many as yet unborn, depend on the continued work of the PHS in catalyzing our national campaign to break the yoke of tobacco.

Second, international health is an area in which the accomplishments of the PHS have been significant but, in my judgment, insufficient. One of my predecessors, Surgeon General Thomas Parran, was largely responsible for the founding of the World Health Organization in the 1940s. The PHS was a proud and generous participant in the successful global effort to eradicate smallpox in the 1960s and 1970s. The PHS regularly participates in international relief efforts, having sent delegations, for example, to work with refugees in Southeast Asia, famine in Africa, and earthquakes in Central America, to cite but a few. Yet the PHS has never had a strong, coherent, and well-funded international health policy that would put our considerable resources to work not only for intermittent initiatives but for consistent health development work. What is needed is an International Health Development Corps within the PHS that would be able to provide technical counsel and support to ministries of health all over the world in a fashion similar to the assistance rendered by the PHS over the years to state and local health departments in this country. Such a program would blend the best traditions of American science and humanitarianism and would be an asset not only to our national health policy but to our foreign policy as well.

Third, the PHS must continue to champion the needs and the rights of the disenfranchised and the forgotten. Handicapped children, the elderly, and those in need of organ transplants are three such groups with whom we have worked hard in recent years. This, though, is the tradition of the PHS starting with its earliest mission—the care of merchant seamen who, prior to the advent of Marine Hospitals, were medically destitute. Early research and treatment of drug addicts, the care of Native Americans, and the National Health Service Corps are all manifestations of the PHS tradition that embraces those whom society as a whole has not. AIDS is the most recent example of this phenomenon and, despite the disinclination of some communities and some public leaders to face the epidemic, the PHS has proceeded with research and public education that emphasizes knowledge, behavior change, and tolerance. The PHS must continue to serve as doctor, investigator and, where possible, helpmate to America's vulnerable whether their numbers are small (ventilator-dependent children) or large (poor children). This will be a hard but noble job.

As the Commissioned Corps begins its second century of service to America and as the PHS as a whole approaches its third, I would like to salute the labors of all federal public health workers, scientists and clinicians, administrators and support staff, commissioned and civilian. I came to the PHS in 1981 after almost forty years as a practicing academic surgeon, arriving with a keen, even critical, objective eye. What I found was enormously exciting. The breadth of the PHS, the professionalism and compassion of its staff, and the responsiveness of its programs have made me proud to serve as Surgeon General.

Plagues and Politics sets the stage for the PHS of today and provides insight into the PHS of the future. It is an important story and one of which I am honored to have been a part.

C. Everett Koop
Surgeon General,
United States Public Health Service

Introduction

History should be, first of all, a good story. This maxim of historical writing came to mind when Surgeon General C. Everett Koop asked me to prepare a historical volume to commemorate the Centennial of the Commissioned Corps of the United States Public Health Service (PHS). The PHS is an agency of the federal government whose policies and programs touch the lives of millions of Americans on a daily basis. Yet its origins as the Marine Hospital Service, its role in immigration and world wars, and its contribution to scientific undertakings as varied as privy building and the space program are little known. The story of the PHS is a colorful and important one, closely tied to the developing history of the nation as a whole. It is, in all, a good story and one that invites telling. I happily undertook the task.

The project was especially appealing to me because I am a commissioned officer in the PHS, as was my grandfather, Dr. Eugene H. Mullan. I bring great affection for the PHS to the exercise of recording its story—a circumstance that has sustained me in the work but one that presents potential hazards to my role as historian. I have labored to write fairly, trying to understand and convey the shortcomings of the Service as well as its achievements, governed by the Surgeon General's only directive—to tell the story well. It must be emphasized, though, that the narrative and interpretations in the book are my own and in no way represent formal policies or positions of the PHS or the federal government.

The history of the PHS is a dramatic one—one of diseases and personalities, of geography and technology. There were, it transpired, photographs to be found in many places which would help to convey this drama. Even though 1989 is the one hundredth anniversary of the Commissioned Corps, it was an act of Congress in 1798 "to provide for the relief of sick and disabled seamen" that initiated federal public health programs. The story certainly had to begin then. While the Commissioned Corps has been central to the work of the Service since 1889, the majority of PHS personnel have always been civil service employees and not commissioned officers. I concluded, therefore, that a narrow history of the Commissioned Corps would neither be good history nor be fair to the people of the PHS. In consequence, *Plagues and Politics* has emerged as a volume rich in photographs, telling the story of the PHS as a whole from its earliest roots to January of 1989.

The PHS has not received a great deal of scholarly or, for that matter, journalistic attention in recent years. Fortunately, two volumes exist (Ralph C. Williams' *The United States Public Health Service 1798-1950* and Bess Furman's *A Profile of the United States Public*

Health Service 1798-1948) that trace the history of the Service to the mid-20th century. These works were of great help to me. Although relatively little has been written about the last forty years, many of the people who have led the PHS over this period are alive and available. I set about collecting oral histories—twenty-one in all, from a variety of people including six Surgeons General and eight Assistant Secretaries for Health. As I looked further, I found and used many works that treated various elements of the history of the PHS and contributed to an understanding of it.

Plagues and Politics proceeds chronologically, letting the events of America's history provide the context for the story as, indeed, they did for the work of the PHS itself. There are, nevertheless, a number of themes in the activities of the PHS that stand out over time—health care, biomedical research, disease control, health protection, and health education. The provision of health care is the oldest role of the Service, existing for many years in the marine hospitals and extant today in the work of the Indian Health Service, the Health Resources and Services Administration (HRSA), and the Alcohol, Drug Abuse and Mental Health Administration (ADAMHA). Biomedical research began in a one room "Laboratory of Hygiene" in 1887 and is now embodied in the National Institutes of Health (NIH), arguably the world's most successful scientific research institution. PHS disease control activities started with quarantine and immigration work at the end of the last century and are manifest today in the programs of the Centers for Disease Control. Since the Pure Food Act of 1906 and still today, health protection has been the statutory mission of the Food and Drug Administration. Public education, though present in virtually all PHS activities, has been the special domain of the Surgeons General—a tradition borne high by Dr. Koop.

Plagues and Politics raises questions for the PHS—questions that are rooted in the past but whose answers are, really, the public health history of the future. In what directions will the PHS develop as health becomes an ever more important national issue? Within the PHS, what is the proper balance between support for health services and support for research—those two ambitious and contentious siblings? What should the posture of the PHS be toward state and local health departments—aloof or engaged, night watchman or den mother? And, finally, the Centennial question: what will be the role of the Commissioned Corps in the next century?

In sum, this is a volume of celebration. I have become convinced in writing it that the history of the PHS invites a great deal more exploration and scholarship. I would hope that this is but the first of a number of monographs on the history of federal public health to be stimulated by the occasions of the Centennial of the Commissioned Corps and the Bicentennial of the PHS in 1998.

Plagues and Politics would not have come to be without the extraordinary participation of many people. Janet Brady Joy has worked with me from the outset as my colleague and photographic research associate, examining thousands of prints and photographs from the collections of the National Library of Medicine, the National Archives, the Smithsonian Institution, the Library of Congress, and the agencies of the PHS. During this time, she corresponded with dozens of present and former PHS officers who offered their photos and memorabilia for use in the book. She collected more than 1,000 images of the PHS, some 200 of which appear on these pages. Her wonderful sense of visual history is present throughout the book.

David Roland, a man with a rare sense of business *and* art, produced the book and served as managing editor, shepherding it from concept to publication. Charles Hyman designed the volume, a magnificent contribution that speaks for itself. The vision and support of Surgeon General Koop, Deputy Surgeon General Faye Abdellah, and Assistant Surgeon General Edward Martin made the book possible. My wife, Judy Mullan, our children, Meghan, Jason, and Caitlin, are owed gratitude and apologies for the many hours they contributed to the book by doing without me. I am grateful for the support and assistance of Martin Kessler and Steve Fraser of Basic Books, Inc. Sarah Bachman, Glenna Crooks, Tom Donnelly, Daniel Fox, Peter Hirtle, Lucinda Keister, Elizabeth Matt, Tom Monath, Hugh Mullan, and Anne Norman all rendered special services to the production of this volume and deserve special thanks. The Commissioned Officers Association of the United States Public Health Service, Johnson and Johnson, Lederle Laboratories, Pfizer Pharmaceuticals, and the Upjohn Co. extended special and timely support to the history project when it was most needed and, thereby, made the book possible. My particular gratitude is due to the National Library of Medicine—a wonderful institution that provided me with a base from which to research and write *Plagues and Politics*.

The members of the Surgeon General's Historical Advisory Committee rendered counsel of enormous value. Many of them read and criticized drafts of the manuscript as it progressed. The Committee members are: Faye Abdellah, Baruch Blumberg, Gert Brieger, Paul Dickson, Paul Ehrlich, Daniel Fox, Marlene Haffner, Victoria Harden, George Hardy, John Kelso, Ramunas Kondratas, Truman McCasland, Carl Merril, Marc Micozzi, John Parascandola, Robert Trachtenberg, Geswaldo Verrone, Suzanne White, and Richard Wyatt.

As mentioned, I undertook oral history interviews with all of the living Surgeons General—Drs. Leonard Scheele, Leroy Burney, William Stewart, Jesse Steinfeld, Julius Richmond and C. Everett Koop—and all of the Assistant Secretaries for Health who have served since the reorganization of 1967—Drs. Philip Lee, Roger Egeberg, Merlin DuVal, Charles Edwards, Theodore Cooper, Edward Brandt, and Robert Windom. W. Palmer Dearing, John Eason, Paul Ehrlich, Tom Hatch, John Kelso, Edward Martin, Charles Miller, and George Silver were also kind enough to grant me lengthy interviews. These wonderful discussions taught me a great deal about the modern PHS, much of which is reflected in the latter chapters of this volume. The interviews are all deposited in the Commissioned Corps Centennial Archive at the History of Medicine Division, National Library of Medicine, Bethesda, Maryland.

Plain and warm thanks are due to the following people: Leonard Bachman, George Baer, Alvin Barnes, John Bartko, Henrietta Bell, Donald Berreth, William Betts, Carolyn Blackwood, Alberta Bourn, Charles Bowman, Jeanne Brand, Allen Brands, Ernie Branson, Merlin Brubaker, Pamela Brye, Robert Burns, J. W. Cashman, Dan Cesari, Bruce Chelikowsky, George Coehlo, Murray Cohen, Marlene Cole, Dale Connelly, Don Cook, W. Clark Cooper, Aleta Cress, Madeline Crisci, Regan Crump, Elizabeth Cunningham, James Curran, Jeanie Daves, Lila Davis, Winston Dean, Patricia DeAsis, Thomas DeCillis, Mary Jo Deering, Nancy Devlin, Raymond Dieter, Jr., James Doherty, Daphine Doster, Mrs. Henry Doyle, Ricardo Dreyfuss, John Duffy, Leonard Dworsky, John Eason, Charles Edwards, Regina el Arculli, Mrs. Paul T. Erickson, Elizabeth Etheridge, John Fanning, Robert Fischer, Nick Fleischer, Wilford Forbush, Kirk Foster, John Freymann, Roy Fritz, Joseph Garcia, Susan Gerhold, Wesley Gilbertson, Joseph H. Goldberger, Martin Goldenberg, Jim Gordon, Victor Haas, Helen Hanlon, Michael Harris, Peter Hartsock, Joseph Hayden, Arthur Hayes, Nancy Hazelton, William Helfand, O. Marie Henry, Lynn Herring, Ina Heyman, William Holcomb, Barbara Horn, O. Jane Hunt, Phyllis Jackson, Wallace Jansen, Warren Johnston, Robert Joy, Margaret Kaiser, Stuart Kaufman, Jeffrey Koplan, Ronald Kostraba, Alan Kraut, Howard Kroll, Jan Lazarus, Sylvia Lee, Mildred Lehman, Nelson Leidel, Pong Lem, Carl Leukefeld, Preston Littleton, Ed Long, Mrs. Santiago Lowergard, Sarah MacArthur, Stuart Mackler, James Maddux, Eamon Magee, Marcia Meyer, Jerrold Michael, J. Donald Millar, Joe Mingiole, Thomas Monath, Marco Montoya, George Moore, Steven Moore, Anthony Mullan, Melvin Myers, Kaarlo Nasi, Philip Nieburg, Roger Nelson, Gary Noble, Paris Pacchione, Ralph Palange, Lowell Peart, Mary Lou Pengelly, James Peters, James Pittman, Laurence Platt, Ralph Porges, Mary Porvaznik, Alex Potter, Mike Randolph, Janice Rary, William Raub, Meribeth Reed, Sylvia Rhoades, Richard Riseberg, Janice Roland, David Shively, Samuel Simmons, Ray Sinclair, Clara Soter, Natalie Davis Spingarn, Thomas Stenvig, Janet Stevens, Angelita Sunga, Richard Taffet, Marian Tebben, Richard Thurm, John Todd, Anne Toohey, Klára Vida, John Villforth, Susan Volkmar, Arlene Waldhaus, James Walker, George Walter, Paul Weinstein, John Weisburger, Paul White, Daniel Whiteside, Robert Whitney, Michael Wilcox, Charles Williams, Larry Wisman, Robert Zobel. To anyone whose contribution I have inadvertently neglected, my apologies and thanks.

Fitzhugh Mullan

Sailors, Sinecures, and Reform

The United States Public Health Service did not begin as an institution dedicated to public health. In fact, the concept of public health as it is known in the late 20th century did not exist when the First Congress met in 1788 and appointed a committee to consider "a bill or bills providing for the establishment of hospitals for sick and disabled seamen".[1]

Late 18th century medicine in the American colonies was limited and notions of a collective response to the challenges of disease—public health—were rudimentary. Efforts at quarantine to deal with periodic outbreaks of epidemic disease, for instance, were hampered by the mystery of etiology—a mystery not to be solved for almost 100 years.

The origins of the Public Health Service are to be found, rather, with sailors and with medical care. The arrival in port cities of merchant seamen, many of whom were ill and unattached, created a burden on public hospitals where they existed and offended public sensibilities everywhere. There was at the time an Anglo-American tradition of public provision for the care of mariners dating from the 16th century triumph of the British Navy over the Spanish Armada. In appreciation, a hospital was built for members of the Royal Navy and, in time, various systems for the welfare of sailors were developed. In the colonies, North Carolina and Virginia had already passed such measures by the time Congress began its deliberations.[2]

It was not until July 16, 1798 that the Fifth Congress passed an Act, signed by President John Adams, providing for

> the temporary relief and maintenance of sick or disabled seamen in the hospitals or other proper institutions now established in the several ports of the United States, or in ports where no such institutions exist, then in such other manner as he (the Secretary of the Treasury) shall direct.[3]

The Act was clearer about the source of the revenue which was to be a charge of twenty cents a month made against the wages of all American sailors than it was about the form of the care. The President was to appoint "directors of the marine hospital of the United States" in the various ports "to provide for the accommodation of sick and disabled seamen." In effect, the law made provisions for a locally collected and administered Marine Hospital Fund that was to be subject to the politics and practices in each port. A law passed in 1799 made naval officers, seamen, and marines beneficiaries of the Marine Hospital Fund, with the secretary of the navy making the pay deductions

The uniform and regalia (opposite) of the Surgeon General of the United States Public Health Service. This was the uniform of Surgeon General Hugh Cumming who served from 1920 to 1936 during which time the position carried two stars. Today it carries three.

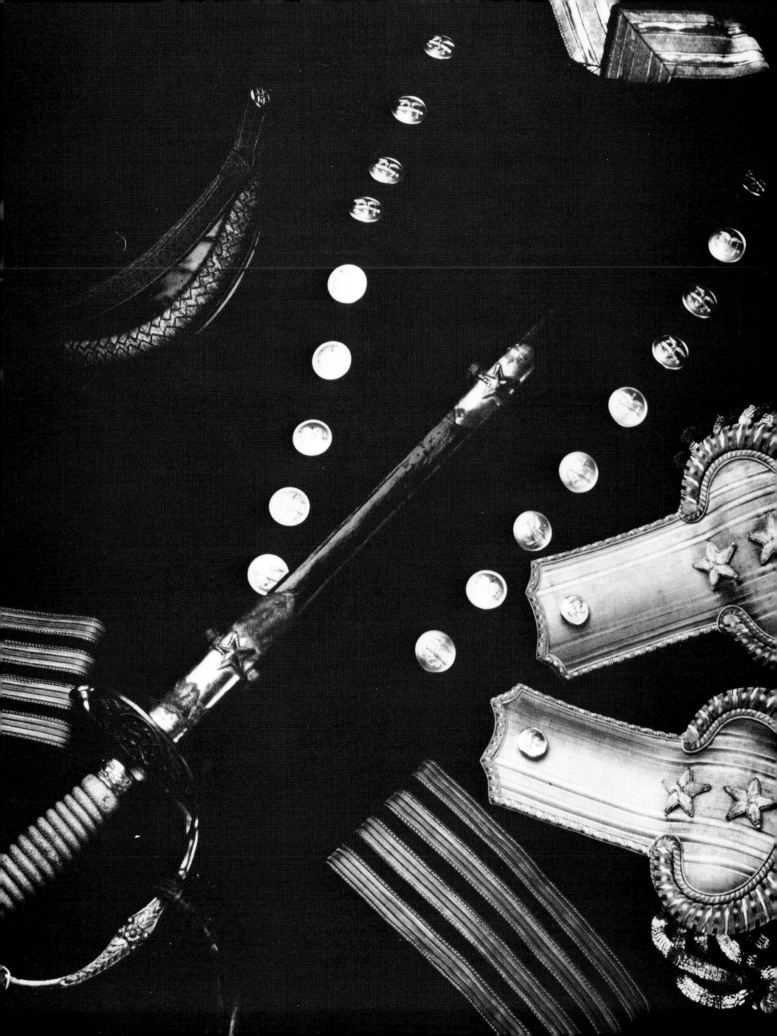

when, in his opinion, a sufficient fund shall be accumulated, he is hereby authorized to purchase or receive cessions or donations of ground, or buildings, in the name of the United States, and to cause buildings, when

necessary, to be erected as hospitals for the accommodation of sick and disabled seamen.

Sec 5. And be it further enacted, That the President of the United States be, and he is hereby authorized to nominate and appoint, in such ports of the United States as he may think proper,

one or more persons, to be called directors of the marine hospital of the United States, whose duty it shall be to direct the expenditure of the fund aforesaid for their respective ports, according to the third section of this act,

to provide for the accommodation of sick and disabled seamen, under such general instructions as shall be given by the President of the United States, for that purpose, and also subject to the like general or

instructions, to direct and govern such hospitals as the President may direct to be built in the respective ports : — and that the said directors shall hold their offices during the pleasure of the President, who is

authorized to fill up all vacancies that may be occasioned by the death or removal of any of the persons so to be appointed. — And the said directors shall render an account of the monies received and expended by

them, once in every quarter of a year, to the Secretary of the Treasury, or such other person as the President shall direct ; but no other allowance or compensation shall be made to the said directors, except

the payment of such expenses as they may incur in the actual discharge of the duties required by this act.

Jonathan Dayton Speaker of the House of Representatives.

Theodore Sedgwick President of the Senate, pro tempore.

Approved July 16. 1798

John Adams

President of the United States.

I certify that this act did originate in

the House of Representatives.

Jonathan W. Condy Clerk

16

and contributions, a circumstance that endured until 1811 when the Navy started its own hospital system.[4]

The hospitals were much needed. "A great number of American citizens, especially seamen and boatmen from the Ohio, die here, yearly," wrote a resident of New Orleans in 1801,

for want of a hospital into which they might be put and taken care of—not that they are refused admittance into the Spanish poor hospital, but that building is by much too small for the purpose. No public house of any reputation will take them in, and consequently they lie in their ships or boats, or get into wretched cabins, in which they die miserably.[5]

The first hospital fully dedicated to the care of merchant sailors was a building purchased at Washington Point, near Norfolk, Virginia in 1801. The first institution actually built with Marine Hospital funds, though, was in Boston harbor. In 1799, the secretary of the treasury, Oliver Wolcott, wrote to the collector of customs of the port of Boston urging him to build a Marine Hospital and recommending a site in the harbor known as Castle Island that had been used as a fort in the days of the Puritans and had housed both British and American troops during the Revolutionary War. The customs collector did as instructed, appointing Dr. Thomas Welsh, a physician with a strong military and political pedigree, as the "Physician to the Hospital." Welsh was forty-eight years old at the time, a graduate of Harvard College who had studied medicine locally and had participated in the battles of Lexington and Bunker Hill. He was a founder of the Massachusetts Medical Society and a member of the American Academy of Arts and Sciences.[6]

Welsh admitted his first charges to a barracks on Castle Island in 1799, defining eligible patients as "All officers of the Navy and of the Marines and all seamen and marines in the public service of the United States, and all officers and seamen in the merchant service". In March of 1800, the secretary of the treasury wrote that the president had approved Welsh's regulations for the hospital which, among other things, described the daily diet in detail, forbade gambling, and required that convalescing patients perform "such reasonable service as the surgeon shall direct." A new facility was opened in the Charlestown section of Boston in 1802, by which time hospitals were also operating in Newport and Charleston in addition to Norfolk.

As the nation grew west, the Mississippi and Ohio Rivers became critical to the nation's commerce and hospitals were constructed in New Orleans and at lake and river cities such as Chicago, Cleveland, St. Louis, and Louisville as well as smaller ports such as Napoleon, Arkansas, and Paducah, Kentucky. All manner of com-

On July 16, 1798, President John Adams (opposite above) signed An Act for the Relief of Sick and Disabled Seamen (opposite below) that provided for a tax of twenty cents a month on the salaries of sailors. The proceeds from this tax were to be used to construct marine hospitals and render care to merchant seamen.

The SEAMEN'S RETREAT HOSPITAL being now entirely free from debt, the Trustees are enabled to offer to the merchant marine the following schedule of reduced fees, viz.:

For Steamships,............$15.00 each Voyage,
" Ships,.................. 11.00 " "
" Barks,................. 9.00 " "
" Brigs,................. 7.00 " "
" Schooners, ... 6.00 " "

The Hospital is located at STAPLETON, STATEN ISLAND, and is a fine, large, airy building, amply furnished for the proper care of sick or disabled seamen, and is devoted exclusively to their treatment--none but seamen being admitted.

This Marine Hospital at Boston harbor (above) was the first built entirely with revenues from the Marine Hospital Fund. In the 1830s, the state of New York established a fund of its own in support of the Seaman's Retreat Hospital on Staten Island for which a tariff was charged (opposite right). The mortar and pestle (opposite left) are from a Marine Hospital Service pharmacy.

plaints were treated. In 1836, Dr. Charles H. Stedman reported on 175 cases seen at the Boston hospital during a three month period, in the "hope that in this manner I may draw the attention of physicians towards this institution." Of this number, venereal diseases were the most prominent with thirty cases of syphilis recorded and eight of gonorrhea. Nineteen had fevers, four had fractured thigh bones and one had a "finger torn off."[7] Several years later, the Boston hospital director, when asked to cut his budget, responded that he could reduce it by half if he were to refuse admission to all those with syphilis and consumption.[8]

Expectations, though, ran well ahead of reality. The care of merchant seamen, as it was organized, was not a system in any contemporary sense of the word but, rather, a loose entitlement managed largely by customs collectors and politicians. Where hospitals were built, they were often crowded or badly staffed and sick seamen were often forced to seek shelter in municipal alms houses. Contract services offered in their stead were frequently unavailable or of poor quality. As early as 1849, complaints about the Fund led to the appointments of Dr. George Loring of the Boston Marine Hospital and Dr. Thomas O. Edwards, a member of Congress from Ohio, to lead a Commission to study the hospitals. Their firm and prescient report concluded that "neither in form nor character has any uniformity in their arrangement been observed" and that a "Chief Surgeon who shall have his bureau attached to the Treasury Department" should be appointed to give central leadership to the hospitals.[9]

Many hospitals, indeed, were built to meet political rather than maritime needs. A Treasury Department report of 1855 complained that, "In some towns there appears a desire . . . (to have Marine Hospitals so) that additional sums of public money may there be expended. If this feeling not be checked, we shall have sinecure surgeons, sinecure stewards, sinecure matrons, sinecure nurses, without number. We have too many such already."[10] The Civil War did nothing to help the state of the Marine Hospitals with the Union and Confederate armies freely occupying them for their own use, converting some to barracks and razing others. Of the twenty-seven hospitals listed before the war, only eight were operational in 1864. In spite of the criticisms and recommendations, national reform or management of the hospitals was not possible due to the absence of any central concept to the program. Throughout this period, for instance, the Marine Revenue Division of the Treasury Department was staffed by but one clerk—the total central administration of the Hospital Fund in Washington.

In 1869, however, Treasury Secretary George S. Boutwell, intent on change, commissioned Dr. W. D. Stewart of his staff and the Army's expert on hospitals, Dr. John Shaw Billings, to travel the country inspecting and reporting on the hospitals. They concluded

The Ship's Medicine Chest

Although an Act of 1790 required every American ship to carry "a chest of medicines, put up by some apothecary of known reputation," the contents of the ship's medicine chest were not specified by law. Enforcement of the regulation by the Department of Commerce was lax, and medicines were frequently depleted or spoiled. In 1876, the Marine Hospital Service began efforts to improve the quality of the printed instructions that accompanied chests. In 1881, under the title "Handbook for the Ship's Medicine Chest," the Marine Hospital Service published the first edition of a volume that eventually became *The Ship's Medicine Chest and First Aid at Sea* and has been carried on U.S. flagged ships ever since. In 1921, the Public Health Service began to provide advice to ships at sea by means of radio and, in 1922, took on responsibility for the design and standardization of ships' medicine chests. Specific lists of medical supplies were drawn up as were blueprints for chests for various types of vessels. *The Ship's Medicine Chest* has been updated regularly over the years, with the latest version being the 500 page, 1984 edition.

simply that "The marine hospital service of the country is upon the whole in an unsatisfactory condition."[11] Of the thirty-one hospitals that had been built since 1798 at a total cost of $3 million, only nine were functioning. Of the balance, two were unfinished, two had been abandoned, one had been transferred to the War Department, one had burned, one had been washed into a river, one was leased, and fourteen had been sold for something less than $400,000. Boutwell proposed legislation that passed in 1870, modifying the marine hospital concept in a slight but critical way, opening the door for enormous change. In addition to a number of minor changes in administration, the position of "Supervising Surgeon of the Marine Hospital Service" was created, setting the stage for the transformation of the ragged Marine Hospital Fund into the disciplined and broad-based Public Health Service of the future.

Key to that evolution, though, was the appointment of Dr. John Maynard Woodworth as the first Supervising Surgeon in April of 1871. Woodworth had studied natural history and medicine in Chicago, graduating from Rush Medical College in 1862 and joining the Union Army. He distinguished himself as General Sherman's chief medical officer in his "March to the Sea," winning several commendations and assimilating the discipline of military medicine that would prove central to his reformation of the Marine Hospital Fund. Billings, who was still an Army officer, worked closely with Boutwell in drafting the 1870 legislation and wanted the job of Supervising Surgeon himself but was blocked by language accompanying the law requiring that the position be filled from "civil life." Thus began a long and destructive contest between two of the early giants of American public health, Woodworth and Billings.

Woodworth moved quickly to transform the Marine Hospital Fund into a true system—the Marine Hospital Service. Starting in 1872, he published annual reports that were crisp, candid and informative. Those reports—as do all other documents of the Service to this day—carried the fouled anchor and caduceus of Mercury, seal of the Service, symbolizing maritime commerce. He moved to close poor facilities, improve contract and outpatient care, and establish nonpolitical, centralized administration of the Service. Patronage had encumbered the marine hospital effort to that point. Woodworth borrowed the military model, which was the only other extant system of appointment to public office in the 1870s, and adapted it to the Service. In 1873, his title was changed to Supervising Surgeon General. From that point, he instituted examinations for all applicants, made appointments only to "the general service" (as opposed to specific locations), and put his new "officers" in uniform. "The importance of this

can scarcely be over estimated," he wrote of his reforms in 1875, "and still, because it is a regulation and not a statutory provision, there are not wanting those who persistently endeavor to break down this barrier against mediocrity and ignorance."[12] The creation of a cadre of competent, mobile, career service physicians in the midst of the Grant administration, noted for graft, and a full decade before the first Civil Service Act was passed in 1883 to check government corruption, stands as an extraordinary feat of public service and administrative reform.

Woodworth's innovations were but one aspect of a period of portentous developments in the nascent discipline of public health. Although some eastern port cities had sponsored municipal health programs to fight epidemics as early as the beginning of the 19th century and Louisiana had briefly empowered a state health agency in 1855, the first permanent state health department was organized in Massachusetts in 1869. A number of states followed suit, intending to put "state medicine," as some called it, to work for the population. The American Public Health Association was founded in 1872, reflecting the growth of interest in hygienic reform and sanitary science. By the mid-1870s, medical leaders, including Doctors Woodworth and Billings, believed that the federal government should play a more active role in the area of public health and should have an agency to embody these expanded functions.

Quarantine, an issue left to the states by statute since the early days of the republic, became the battleground for the contending forces of federal public health expansion. The enforcement of quarantine regulations, inconsistent as they were from locality to locality, was variable and often nonexistent. In 1875, Woodworth character-

Marine Hospital Service Surgeon Trulon V. Miller (above center, seated) designed the Service's first uniform. In this 1878 photo, Miller and his fellow officers at the Chicago Marine Hospital are in regulation clothing. It is the earliest known picture of the first Service uniform, which carried the letters "MD" on the lapel of the blouse in old English script and the Marine Hospital Service seal as a cap ornament. The seal (right), designed by Surgeon General John Maynard Woodworth, consisted of the fouled anchor of maritime life and the double-snaked caduceus of Mercury which symbolized commerce.

ized the federal quarantine law as "a dead letter." A yellow fever epidemic in New Orleans in 1877 that spread quickly up the Mississippi valley riveted national attention on quarantine policy and forced congressional action. The Quarantine Act of 1878 was a victory for the Marine Hospital Service, conferring upon it quarantine authority— its first mission beyond the care of merchant seaman in the eighty years of its existence.

The victory was to be shortlived. Believing that the federal government should have a health agency similar to those appearing on the state and local levels, the American Public Health Association, Billings, and Woodworth all introduced bills in 1879 proposing the establishment of a National Health Department. The acrimonious competition between Billings and Woodworth reached a crescendo in the maneuvering surrounding this legislation with Billings' plan eventually being backed by the American Public Health Association and Woodworth struggling to avoid having the Marine Hospital Service usurped by Billings or the Army. The outcome was the enactment of a National Board of Health to be comprised of nine members appointed by the President, including one each from the Army, Navy, and the Marine Hospital Service. The Service was maintained as an independent agency but all of the quarantine functions of the 1878 Act were transferred to the National Board of Health, curtailing Woodworth's ambitions for his program.

On March 14, 1879, eleven days after the passage of the National Board of Health legislation, John Woodworth died. He was forty-one years old. Little is recorded about his final illness or the cause of death but his legacy is clear. In less than a decade, he had fashioned the Marine Hospital Service out of a handful of dilapidated federal institutions and simultaneously inaugurated a career medical service within the federal government that would prove to be the backbone of federal public health in the 20th century.

Woodworth was quickly succeeded by John B. Hamilton, a thirty-one-year-old physician who, after service in the Union Army, had graduated from Rush Medical College. After several years in private practice in Chicago, he joined the Army Medical Corps and in 1876 resigned to accept an appointment as an Assistant Surgeon in the Marine Hospital Service. He distinguished himself as the officer-in-charge at several marine hospitals before being called to Washington as the Supervising Surgeon General of the Service. New though he was to the ways of the Capital, it was not long before he took up where Woodworth left off in the struggle with Billings.

The National Board of Health set about establishing an active program of public health surveillance and intervention including

John B. Hamilton (above) succeeded Woodworth as Supervising Surgeon General in 1879 and served until 1891. It was during his tenure that the 1889 legislation formalizing the Commissioned Corps was enacted. Quarantine stations, like the one on Staten Island (opposite below), were built outside major ports in an effort to prevent the spread of infectious diseases from incoming vessels. They were often affiliated with marine hospitals and their work was not always popular (opposite above). In the summer of 1858, an angry mob attacked and burned the facility on Staten Island because yellow fever patients were being landed and detained there.

monthly meetings of the Board, grants to states for sanitary work, and the weekly publication of a *Bulletin* reporting on disease outbreaks. (The *Bulletin* had originally been issued by the Marine Hospital Service as a result of the 1878 Quarantine Act and was later to be published by the Public Health Service as *Public Health Reports*.) The aggressiveness of the Board's efforts stimulated states' rights objections in some quarters and a number of jurisdictions opposed its quarantine activities, contributing to its growing political problems. Hamilton missed no opportunity to testify against the Board or plant rumors about the alleged corruption and incompetence of Board members. In the end, the Board foundered on its appropriation which expired on June 30, 1883. Hamilton fought successfully against an extension of the funding and, although the Board remained on the statute books for another decade, it effectively ceased to function in 1883. The Marine Hospital Service resumed its surveillance and quarantine activities which were strengthened by subsequent Quarantine Acts.[13]

Although he was the loser in the struggle over the National Board of Health, Billings went on to a brilliant career which included organizing the Library of the Surgeon General of the Army (now the National Library of Medicine), creating the *Index Medicus*, and designing the Johns Hopkins and Peter Bent Brigham Hospitals. His vision for a national health agency was one that was to recur regularly and one which, per force, always involved the Marine/Public Health Service as the only nonmilitary, federal health agency. Woodworth and Hamilton, as would be the case with their successors, found themselves in a delicate position because, whatever their beliefs about a national health department, their first allegiance was to the Service they superintended. Their political strategy tended to be parochial and put them in opposition to an idea that actually embodied many of the principles to which they and the members of their Service were dedicated. Repeatedly and successfully, the Service would protect itself and its circumscribed mission against proposals for an expanded federal department of health—an agency that might well have provided greater scope for the work of the Service over the long run but would have superceded its position as the government's sole civilian health unit. The early Surgeons General were fiercely loyal to their Service and the historical paradox of their opposition to a national department of health did not trouble them.

The services rendered to sailors expanded rapidly in the years following Woodworth's reforms. The "number of seaman relieved" (in-patient and out-patient visits) grew annually from 10,560 in 1870, to 24,860 in 1880, to 50,671 in 1890.[14] In 1877, Walter Wyman, an officer who would later become Surgeon General, wrote of work on the Mississippi and Ohio Rivers,

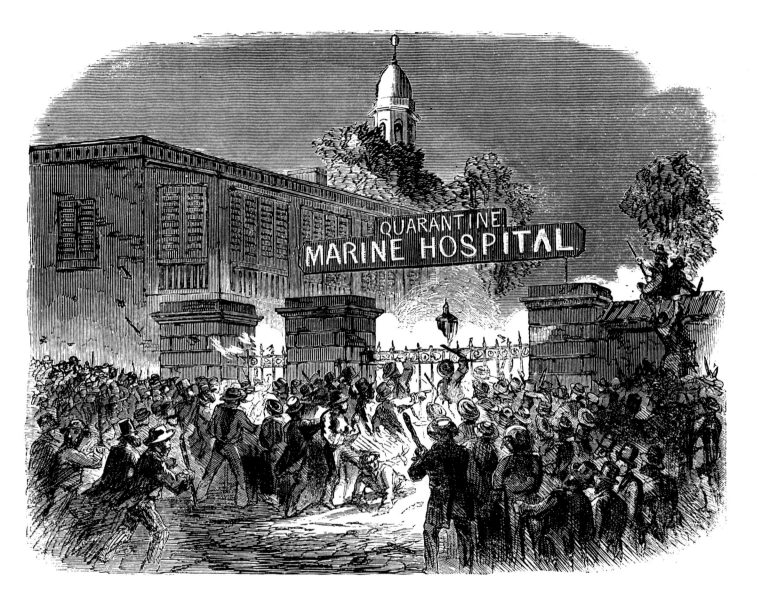

Beginning in 1879, Marine Hospital Service physicians were assigned to serve on vessels of the Revenue-Cutter Service (now the Coast Guard) such as the cutter "Bear" (right). Assistant Surgeon Watkins of the United States Public Health and Marine Hospital Service took this photograph of "Natives & Iglot" (above) in the early years of this century.

It cannot be denied that here and there is a boat on which good shelter is provided and wholesome food furnished in abundance. But such boats are the exceptions, not affecting the general rule. The fact is undisputed that the river-roustabout leads a life of unparalleled hardship.[15]

Trauma and syphilis were particular nemeses of sailors with Woodworth stating flatly in his 1878 report that at least 40 percent of seamen suffered from venereal disease "in one of its protean forms." Large sections of every *Annual Report* were dedicated to case descriptions, with the volume of 1883 reporting on a skull fracture caused by a metal bar thrown from a steam winch, an accidental gunshot wound to the eye, and a contusion of the perineum with lacerations of the urethra suffered as the result of a three-foot fall through an open hatch. Deaths from a vast array of diseases including measles, cerebro-spinal fever, enteric fever, syphilis, and phthisis pulmonalis were recorded that year. The clinical life of the Marine Hospital Service was as robust as maritime life was hazardous.

Surgeon General Woodworth had used the expedient of regulation to make his reforms. Merit appointment, career service, and the use of the uniform were his innovations, backed by the secretary of the treasury, but not enforced by the power of law and therefore subject to the whim of future politicians. By the mid-1880s, the Service was growing in size as well as activities with some fifty officers on duty, up from thirty-one in 1877.[16] The ranks of Assistant Surgeon, Passed Assistant Surgeon and Surgeon had been created within the Service with boards of examination convened twice yearly to scrutinize and select new officers. "The Service is open to all regular graduates in medicine, between the ages of twenty-one and thirty years, without regard to political preferences," Surgeon General Hamilton wrote pointedly in the 1885 *Annual Report*. "This system has been followed since 1873, and has brought into the Service professional qualifications of the highest order."[17]

Imbedded in this statement were several troubling problems for the Service. In undertaking the reforms of 1873, Woodworth had sought to escape the depredations of political patronage that typified not only the early years of the Marine Hospital Fund, but all levels of government in post-Civil War America. Woodworth and Hamilton were determined and successful in their efforts to build a professional corps that would be free of political favoritism and the prevalent spoils system of public life. Additionally, they faced the difficult challenge of professional standards and selection that gave their insistence on competitive exams added importance. American medical schools of the time were large in number, variable in quality, and frequently divided in philosophy. The improvements in the quality and uniformity of medical education that would take place in the early 20th century were still many years in the future, and the revolution of Pasteur and Koch on which those changes would be based was just beginning in

Europe as Woodworth and Hamilton struggled with their reforms.

Early in his tenure, Hamilton set about obtaining legislation that would give the Service a strength and permanency that Woodworth's regulations alone could not ensure. He addressed his concerns about both the substantive and the political importance of examinations to the secretary of the treasury in 1885, stating that the Service's exams were practically oriented and required "an acquaintance with the English branches of a common school education," as well as chemistry, anatomy, physiology, "and the most intimate knowledge of the practical professional branches." He continued,

> It is difficult to imagine that a man of experience would seriously urge the appointing power to cause the setting aside of regulations so obviously in the interest of humanity, simply to obtain a place for a friend however needy, but experience has convinced me that nothing short of a law will prevent these attempts with each recurring change of administration, and I firmly believe that, although the merit system may be temporarily overshadowed, it will ultimately prevail and become firmly established.[18]

Hamilton was clear that he wanted a law to establish formally a Commissioned Corps of the Marine Hospital Service and to provide the stability and protection he felt the Service needed. His campaign

When yellow fever again became epidemic in 1888, the Marine Hospital Service detained people suspected of having the disease at Camp E. A. Perry (below) near the Florida-Alabama border. The three women (opposite), Misses Bullard, Ferguson, and Norsdorff, were nurses employed by the Service for duty in a yellow fever camp in Franklin, Louisiana, during an outbreak in 1898.

succeeded when, on January 4, 1889, President Grover Cleveland signed *An Act to Regulate Appointments in the Marine Hospital Service of the United States.* In two simple sections, this Act put the reforms of the previous years into law, specifying that the medical officers of the Marine Hospital Service would thereafter be appointed by the president with the advice and consent of the Senate after passing "a satisfactory" examination.

The Marine Hospital Service and its Commissioned Corps had thus positioned itself for the explosion in biological knowledge and sanitary reform activity that was to come in the ensuing decades. Hamilton, it would seem, had an inkling of the future when, fresh from victory in the National Board of Health battle and ambitious for the future of the Service, he began a quiet campaign to have the name of the Service changed to the Public Health Service. It would be a number of years later and after his death that the name change would occur, but the transformation of the narrowly based Marine Hospital Service into a wide-ranging institution whose programs would touch every aspect of American life, was well underway before the sudden resignation of John Hamilton as Surgeon General in June of 1891.

Science, Immigrants, and the Public Health Movement

The last decades of the 19th century were years of enormous scientific ferment and prodigious biological discovery. The early work of Louis Pasteur and Robert Koch pinpointing microorganisms as the causes of specific illnesses opened the way for the rapid identification of the agents of many infectious diseases. Between 1880 and 1900, the mystery of the etiology of such perennial killers as typhoid, tuberculosis, cholera, malaria, leprosy, tetanus, and plague yielded to the probing intelligence of the new science of bacteriology. The recognition of carrier states in cholera, diphtheria, and typhoid as well as the discovery of insect and animal vectors in plague, malaria, and yellow fever rounded out the germ theory of disease and gave physicians and public health workers a vastly improved position in their battle against disease.

In the United States, the bacteriological revolution arrived in a country that had become a true transcontinental nation, where the full economic and social impact of industrialization was just being felt. National wealth was expanding rapidly and helping to lure hundreds of thousands of immigrants to the country every year. Prosperity, though, was not well distributed. At the turn of the century, 2 percent of the population owned 60 percent of the wealth and an estimated 40 percent of seventy-six million Americans were living in conditions of poverty. Population growth proceeded six times as fast in cities as in the countryside, creating tenements, slums, and urban blight in its wake.

Out of these conditions, out of the dissonance between the promise of a democratic, affluent, just America and the reality of an America that was, for many, squalid and inequitable, grew the Progressive Movement. It was characterized by a belief in government as an instrument to better the lot of the governed, embracing the concepts of activism, intervention, and bureaucracy. Not surprisingly, it focused on the poor, the exploited, the ill-represented. Its heroes were social workers and muckrakers, feminists and syndicalists, political reformers and conservationists. Indeed, conservation of human and natural resources was a central theme of Progressivism and an obvious point of commonality with the public health movement that took new strength from the bacteriological revolution. By the early years of the 20th century, public health workers on all levels, armed with new scientific tools, buoyed by the momentum of Progressivism, were prepared to challenge disease on a scale previously unknown.

This young woman (opposite) and many like her were introduced to America at the immigration and quarantine facility on Ellis Island in New York harbor. Between 1890 and 1920, some twenty million would-be Americans passed by the screening eyes and under the examining hands of the Marine Hospital (soon to become Public Health) Service.

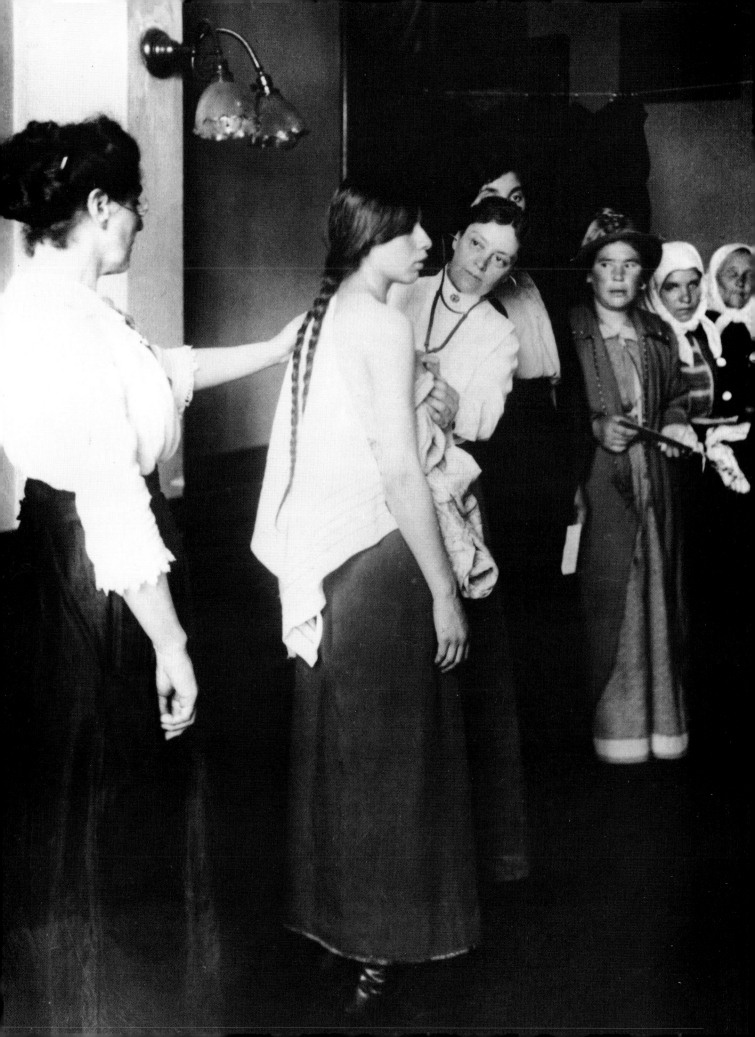

Homes of
the Poor

On the first of June of 1891, John Hamilton left his post as Surgeon General and returned to Chicago as a surgeon at the Marine Hospital there. His reasons for leaving are unclear but President Benjamin Harrison promptly accepted Hamilton's recommendation that he be replaced by Dr. Walter Wyman. Wyman, a native of St. Louis and a graduate of Amherst College and St. Louis Medical College, was forty-two at the time and a fifteen-year veteran of the Marine Hospital Service. A bachelor and a stickler for precision, his tenure in office was characterized by his personal dedication to the Service and its officers as well as indefatigable attention to administrative procedures and the specifics of Service protocol. Reportedly, he examined all of the mail leaving his office for the correctness of the addresses and attended to every detail of the various Service uniforms.

Surgeon General Wyman enjoyed bureaucracy and he built his very effectively. The fifty-four medical officers and $600,000 budget over which he took command in 1891 grew to 135 officers and a budget of $1,750,000 by 1911.[1] Under his careful political guidance, the Congress enlarged the name of the Service in 1902 to the Public Health and Marine Hospital Service and formally eliminated the "Supervising" in the title, Surgeon General. Not only was his meticulous management and penchant for public administration ideally suited to the expansion of his program, but it typified the commitment to bureaucracy that was common to Progressive era institutions.

Joining Wyman at the Service's new headquarters in the Butler Building across the street from the Capitol in Washington in late 1891, was an institution of portent for the future—the Hygienic Laboratory. Opened by direction of Surgeon General Hamilton in 1887 in one room in the Marine Hospital on Staten Island, the Laboratory had engaged in studies of cholera and yellow fever as well as the bacterial content of the waters of the New York Bay. At Staten Island, it was well situated to investigate the illnesses of seamen and immigrants but Hamilton soon realized the potential importance of the Laboratory to the work of the Service as a whole and initiated its move to Washington. From the outset, the Laboratory was directed by Dr. Joseph Kinyoun, a physician who had studied microbiology in New York and practiced medicine for several years with his father in Johnson County, Missouri, before joining the Service in 1886. Because of his training in bacteriology, his initial assignment was to start a "laboratory of hygiene" at the Staten Island Hospital.

The young scientist was ambitious for his new institution, writing shortly after the move to Washington that "The subjects of hygiene and demography have not as yet received the proper amount of attention from our legislative bodies. This laboratory, situated and equipped as it is, should form the nucleus of one national in character, and developed on the same basis as those established in Germany,

Poverty and urban blight (opposite) were the targets of the Progressives and sanitary reformers who collaborated during the early years of the twentieth century to produce a highly effective public health movement. During much of this period, Dr. Walter Wyman (above) served as Surgeon General, overseeing important expansion in the research, quarantine, and immigration activities of the Service and a change in name to the Public Health and Marine Hospital Service.

As early as the 1890s, the Hygienic Laboratory engaged in the production of therapeutic sera and antitoxins (right) and trained scientists from state health departments in these techniques. Legislation passed in 1902 authorized the construction of a new facility for the Hygienic Laboratory (opposite, above and below), which was opened in 1904 in Washington, D.C. at 25th and E streets. The Service's portable laboratories (below) provided the equipment necessary for bacteriological diagnosis of infectious diseases in the field.

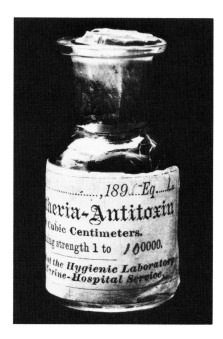

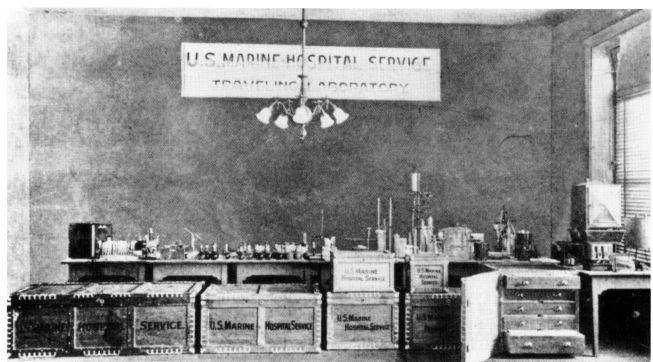

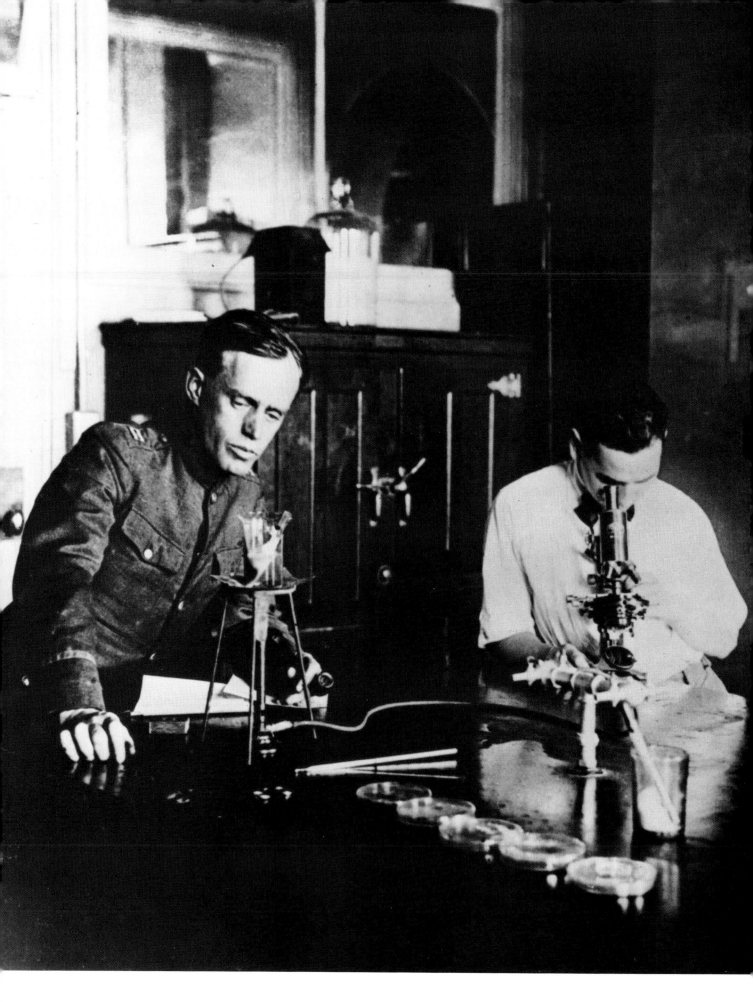

France and England."[2] Kinyoun labored with a small staff, responding to a variety of scientific and political stimuli. In addition to multiple studies on newly identified bacteria, he experimented with disinfectant gases and designed systems to deliver them to the cargo of ships. In 1894, the Congress asked the Laboratory to examine ventilation in the House of Representatives. Kinyoun reported candidly that not only was the air of the Capitol fouled with leaking gas and tobacco smoke, but in some places the carpet was so saturated with tobacco expectoration that it tended "to make it odorous."[3]

The Laboratory began the manufacture of diphtheria antitoxin in the United States in 1894 after Kinyoun travelled to Europe to study the process with Emile Roux of the Pasteur Institute. State and local health officials were brought to the Laboratory for instruction in the new technique, initiating an important tradition of the Laboratory as a training institution. Kinyoun worried, though, that with the publicized success of vaccines and antitoxins, impure or worthless preparations would be sold to an unprotected public. Some government agency, he believed, should regulate the marketing of these highly commercial products. His concerns fed into a larger legislative initiative that resulted in the Biologics Control Act of 1902, giving the Hygienic Laboratory regulatory authority in the production and sale of vaccines and antitoxins. This law was an early and archetypal achievement for health reformers in the Progressive era and its regulatory functions remained an important activity of the Laboratory for some thirty years.[4]

Milton J. Rosenau (above) served as the second director of the Hygienic Laboratory (1899 to 1909) after a number of Service field assignments and before going on to become a leader in academic public health at Harvard. Service physicians and scientists working in the lab (opposite) and in the field made discoveries of disease organisms and vectors that helped to bring many of the scourges of the 19th century under control.

The investigative activities of the Hygienic Laboratory were never far from the front lines of public health practice in those early years. Kinyoun's career, itself, is dramatically illustrative of this point. In 1899, Surgeon General Wyman decided to call Dr. Milton Rosenau, a thirty-year-old officer in charge of the Service's quarantine duties in San Francisco, to Washington to direct the Laboratory and to send Kinyoun to California to assume the quarantine post. The presence of cholera and concern over the possibility of plague that was endemic in Asia and had recently arrived in Hawaii made the San Francisco job a clinically important and politically difficult one. On March 6, 1900, the first case of plague on the North American continent was diagnosed in San Francisco's Chinatown and was followed by many others. Kinyoun confirmed the diagnosis in the Marine Hospital Laboratory and initiated a campaign of quarantine directed at Chinatown and arriving immigrants. The Chinese community opposed his efforts as disruptive and prejudicial and the governor, Henry T. Gage, adopted a policy of denial, stating that there was no plague in California.

For more than a year the battle raged, with Kinyoun seeking the authority to "clean up" Chinatown and impose quarantine measures and Governor Gage leading the press in what one San Francisco physician called "a campaign of vilification . . . that for unexampled bitterness, unfair and dishonest methods, probably never had been and never again will be equalled."[5] In March, 1901, an independent commission concluded that plague, indeed, was present in San Francisco and the state agreed to cooperate with federal officials in combatting the disease on the condition that Kinyoun leave California.

In the following years, local authorities cooperated with the Marine Hospital Service, but plague had established a firm hold in the Bay Area from which it would spread to become endemic in the rodent population of much of the western United States. Kinyoun went on to represent the Service in Japan and Canada before resigning in 1903 to direct a private laboratory.

Under Rosenau, the Hygienic Laboratory prospered. The 1902 law entitled "An act to increase the efficiency and change the name of the United States Marine Hospital Service" specifically added divisions of chemistry, zoology, and pharmacology to the Laboratory whose previous activities had been limited to bacteriology and pathology. The legislation did not provide for the commissioning of non-physician scientists, but did permit them to be hired under the Civil Service as division directors with the title of "Professor," a largely unsatisfactory arrangement that was to last another forty years. The law called for an Advisory Board whose first chairman was to be the great steward of scientific medicine, William Henry Welch of Johns Hopkins, and in 1904, the Laboratory moved to handsome new quarters designed specially for it. Scientific research had taken firm root in the Public Health and Marine Hospital Service.

Bubonic plague appeared for the first time in North America in San Francisco in 1900. Dr. Joseph Kinyoun (above) who had served previously as the director of the Hygienic Laboratory (1887 to 1899) was on assignment in San Francisco and planned a vigorous campaign against plague but was opposed by local politicians who denied the presence of the disease. Plague became endemic in the San Francisco area for a number of years thereafter, necessitating a permanent Service plague laboratory (opposite above). Scientists at the laboratory (opposite below) dissect squirrels and rats for evidence of plague.

The diseases we suffer from are, after all, criminals that attack, rob and murder mankind," wrote Dr. Samuel Grubbs of his Service work. "The public health officer tries to block the roads by which disease reaches his people. He is a 'detective,' a 'federal agent,' employed in the interest of national health."[6] Nowhere was the notion of the Service as medical gatekeeper and protector of the nation more apparent than at America's ports of entry. A series of laws starting in 1891 called on the Service to provide medical inspection of all arriving immigrants and the Quarantine Act of 1893 placed ultimate authority for quarantine enforcement with the Surgeon General rather than with the states. Reflected in the language of the law that prohibited the admission of "idiots, insane persons, . . . persons likely to become a public charge, (and) persons suffering from a loathsome or a dangerous contagious disease" was a particular concern with infectious disease and public charity. The Commissioner General of Immigration, Terence Powderly, put it

succinctly in 1902 when he stated that America should not be allowed to become "the hospital of the nations of the earth."[7] It was the job of the Service to defend against the risks of the wide open immigration policy of those years and, above all, to exclude those who were "lpc"—likely to become a public charge. It is for this reason that mental illness and mental retardation as well as trachoma (because of its tendency to cause blindness) were particular targets of the screening activities of the Service.

Although the Service staffed immigration stations on all the nation's borders, New York was the magnet for most European immigration with almost two-thirds of each year's new arrivals debarking there. Incoming ships were boarded by state and federal officials who checked for "germ diseases"—typhus, cholera, plague, smallpox, and yellow fever—and quickly certified the health of cabin passengers. Immigrants in third class and steerage were then ferried to what was called "The Island of Hope" and also "The Island of Tears"—Ellis Island. Ellis Island was, in fact, three small, adjacent islands on which were built an administration and detention building, a general hospital, and a communicable disease hospital. Ellis Island constituted a

The Service fought the battle against plague outside the laboratory as well. Ground squirrels that might carry the disease were destroyed (below) in the San Francisco East Bay area, and energetic cleanup campaigns were launched in an effort to find and eliminate rats. The house (opposite) has been raised for ratproofing.

standing challenge for the Service since the number of medical officers assigned there was never great, increasing from six in 1892 to twenty-five in 1915. In addition to boarding arriving ships and running the two hospitals, they were charged with screening almost a million immigrants a year who often arrived in groups as large as 5,000 a day. Their solution was a blend of science and bureaucracy.

The principle developed was "The Line"—the systematic, rapid observation of ambulatory immigrants by seasoned observers, fluent in a few phrases of a dozen languages. The minority of immigrants thus identified as physically or mentally suspicious were set aside for more careful exams while the majority were sent on to the Immigration Service. The Line began for the newcomers when they climbed a flight of stairs to get to the main hall of the arrival building, watched carefully by a medical officer scrutinizing posture and gait, and looking for signs of debility or shortness of breath.

Four lines then proceeded from that point, each superintended by a physician observing the passing men, women, and children at close quarters. "As the immigrant approaches, the officer gives him a quick glance," wrote Eugene H. Mullan of his work on The Line. "Experience enables him in that one glance to take in six details, namely, the scalp, face, neck, hands, gait, and general condition, both mental and physical."[8] The four lines terminated in front of two physicians who performed eye examinations looking specifically for trachoma. Any abnormality deemed worthy of further investigation was noted by a chalk mark made by the officer on the immigrant's clothing, a C for conjunctivitis, CT for trachoma, G for goiter, H for heart, X for mental defect, and so forth. The marked individuals left The Line and were shown by an attendant to the Service's examination area. The others continued on to the Immigration Service.

Some 15 to 20 percent were chalked and held by the Public Health Service for further scrutiny. Overall, something less than one percent were finally denied entry into the United States but those must have been painful events for everyone involved. Dr. Victor Heiser described the experience thus:

A Scandinavian farmer might spend years in Minnesota earning enough money to pay the passage for his wife and their five children. When they would finally arrive, and the long separated family would be reunited, ours would be the painful duty of singling out one of the children, and of saying, "She has trachoma. She cannot enter." The mother and the rest of the children would often have to return to Europe with the diseased one, and, until the boat sailed, the father, wretched and unhappy, would haunt the detention quarters, while his family kept up a constant wailing and crying.[9]

The officers of the Public Health Service, uniformed and disciplined as they were, constituted the immigrant's first contact with Americans in America. It is not hard to imagine that many were intimidated by the martial quality of a process that they little under-

In 1908, The San Francisco Citizens' Health Committee sponsored a luncheon (opposite above) commemorating the completion of the plague control campaign, whose slogan was "San Francisco is so clean, a meal can be eaten in the streets." Dr. Rupert Blue, who led the campaign and later became Surgeon General, was the guest of honor. When plague appeared in New Orleans in 1914, the Service drew on its San Francisco experience. A squad of rat trappers (opposite below) poses with the instruments of their trade.

stood in a setting where they were often unable to talk with their examiners for lack of a common language. Many interviewed in later years thought they had been greeted by soldiers, surely an upsetting misinterpretation. Yet the Public Health Service record is, overall, one of fairness and efficiency. The practice of Service officers was to segregate their role as doctors examining and treating individuals from the requirements of the nation for social control over those arriving on its shores.

This was not easily done. The agitation of "Nativists" pressing for much more restrictive laws and policies was considerable. The job of the Service officers was to make medical diagnoses for the use of the Immigration Service and those who made immigration policy but not to function as arbiters themselves. In this spirit, Service physicians never sat on the Boards of Special Inquiry that made the final decision on exclusions and, at a number of points, the Service resisted

Quarantine duty included the inspection of incoming ships. Service physicians accompanied harbor pilots meeting arriving vessels and examined the ship, its passengers, and crew on the way to port. The officer (opposite) has left the launch and is scaling the Jacob's ladder to the ship's deck. Fumigation was used (below) on vessels where evidence of "excessive" numbers of rats was found, and on those arriving from ports known to be plague infested.

Huge steam chambers such as these (above) were used to disinfect immigrants' baggage at their home ports. The travelers themselves took showers and were deloused before they were permitted to embark for the new world. Immigrants from Asia arriving in San Francisco debarked at Angel Island (opposite above). Two-thirds of the new arrivals came through what was known as the Island of Hope, Ellis Island in New York harbor (opposite below). In addition to screening as many as 5,000 immigrants a day, Service officers stationed at Ellis Island ran two hospitals and inspected all vessels arriving from foreign ports.

pressure from the Immigration Service to find more of the arrivals physically or mentally unfit. Moreover, the Service did not suffer from graft and favoritism, as was documented from time to time with the Immigration Service.[10] The white, male, predominantly southern, physicians of the Public Health and Marine Hospital Service were certainly liable to a variety of cultural biases, but given the press of newcomers, the demands of Nativists, and the paucity of their own numbers, they served as evenhanded—even benevolent keepers of the gate. In all, almost twenty million immigrants passed under their examining eyes from 1891 to 1924, making them midwives, of a sort, to the American nation.

Although the Law of 1893 passed the baton of quarantine authority to the federal government, public health activity in general remained the domain of the states. Responding much as the federal government had, state boards of health grew up throughout the country in the late 19th century with forty of the forty-five states having designated health authorities by 1902. The Act of 1902 that changed the name of the Service to the Public Health and Marine Hospital Service contained critical provisions that quietly bound federal and state public health activities together and put the Surgeon General at the head of the growing public health movement. The legislation charged him with convening a conference of state health authorities on an annual basis or "whenever in his opinion the interest of the public health would be promoted by such a conference." Five or more state health officers, likewise, could require the Surgeon General to call the group into session to discuss a public health emergency.

The new law also directed the Surgeon General to prepare and distribute to state health officers "suitable and necessary" forms for the uniform compilation of information on births, deaths, and specified diseases and that this information be published in the journal of the Service, *Public Health Reports*. "There is little doubt," wrote Wyman in his Annual Report of 1902, "that (much) may be developed out of the law in coordinating the labors of the national and state health authorities . . . ."[11] The contentiousness that had marked state and federal public health dealings and was typified by Kinyoun's California plague battle was dissipated by the 1902 legislation and the relationships that evolved from it. Fostered by annual meetings as well as special sessions dealing with threats such as plague and cholera, the collegiality that developed between the Service and state health officials became the bedrock of public health practice in the United States for the next fifty years.

Cooperation between the Public Health Service and state governments occasionally took the form of specific assignments. In 1914,

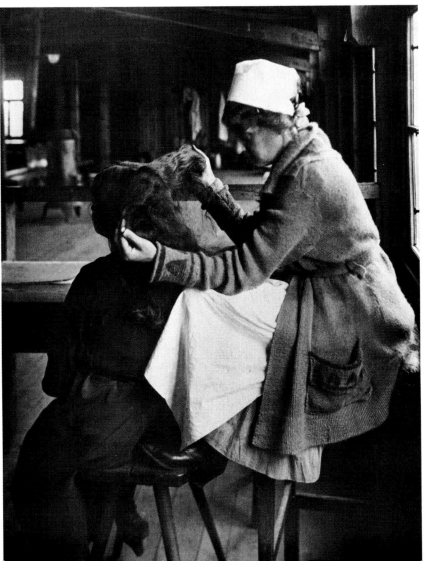

At all ports of entry into the United States, the Service was charged with the inspection of arriving immigrants. Service physicians screened every prospective citizen, observing them as they passed along "The Line." A specially constructed example of this was the night inspection room (opposite above) at the New Orleans Quarantine Inspection Station. It was painted and artificially lighted to approximate daylight. A medical officer (opposite below) looks for evidence of trachoma, a highly contagious eye disease. Its detection meant certain rejection. Mental deficiencies were often difficult to ascertain because of language barriers. A woman (above) works a puzzle as part of one test. Some immigrants were inspected under Service supervision in their home countries before embarking for the United States. The young Irish woman (left) had gone through a delousing procedure and her hair is being inspected to make sure that no unwelcome travelers came to the new country with her.

2. AMESS
3. WHITE
4. Gov BLANCHARD
5. BLUE
6. McMULLEN
7. CURRIE
8. McKLON
9. ASHFORD
10. DE VALIN

12. RICHA
13. GOLDBE
14. CORPUT
15. EBERT
16. RUCKE
17. STEGA
18. GUTHR
19. FROST

Officers of the Public Health and Marine Hospital Service who took part in a campaign against yellow fever in New Orleans in 1905 sit for their portraits (above) with the governor of Louisiana. In the group are a number of officers who went on to distinguished careers, including future Surgeon General Rupert Blue (fifth from left, seated) and Joseph Goldberger (fourth from left, middle row). A newly-commissioned Assistant Surgeon, Eugene H. Mullan (right), also participated in the yellow fever work in New Orleans in 1905. In a rare glimpse of Service family life, Samuel Grubbs (opposite) poses with his son, circa 1906.

Life in the Service

L ife in the Service had a quality and cadence of its own, beginning with a monumental examination that most applicants failed. Dr. Victor Heiser chronicled the experience of forty-two young physicians who arrived with him in Washington in the summer of 1898. After a physical exam eliminated some, the remaining thirty candidates began a week's ordeal of written tests. Every morning, some of their number were quietly dismissed, increasing the pressure on those who continued. Evenings were devoted to study.

It was July in Washington. I would sit in my room with no clothes on, and, even though the windows and transom were open, the perspiration would run off me in streams. At three o'clock I would tumble into bed and reluctantly out at eight in time for a bath and breakfast before the torture began again.

Ten remained for the oral "pre-medical" exam where they were queried on their knowledge of the world, including, typically, a request to read aloud in French or discourse on the Rosetta Stone. The final hurdle was clinical. Heiser and his remaining colleagues visited a local hospital where they were required to examine and diagnose six patients and identify bacteria and parasites under the microscope. Eight fatigued applicants completed this ordeal. Two weeks later, three, including Heiser, received letters offering them commissions in the Service.

The work of the Service was often hazardous. John Branham, a Georgian, graduated from medical school in Baltimore, was commissioned in April of 1893 and assigned to the Staten Island Marine Hospital. In June of that year, the captain of an American ship arriving on the Georgia coast from Cuba became sick, went ashore and died of yellow fever. On July 20, President Grover Cleveland approved the Surgeon General's request to federalize the quarantine activities in Georgia and sent Branham to take charge. A month later, after ten days of illness, Branham was dead, the sixth Marine Hospital medical officer to succumb to yellow fever in fifteen years. Surgeon General Wyman eulogized Branham in the *Annual Report* of 1894 and a bill was introduced in Congress authorizing $4,160 (two years' salary) "For the Relief of the Family of the Late Assistant Surgeon John Branham." Four years later, the Act was passed.

For many, the Service was a culture, a way of life that entailed work, frequent moves, a far-flung camaraderie with other officers, and a quiet, perennial commitment to national service. In the spring of 1897, a twenty-six year-old physician named Samuel B. Grubbs joined the Service. Almost half a cen-

tury later, he described that culture in his autobiography entitled *By Order of the Surgeon General: Thirty-seven Years of Active Duty in the Public Health Service.*

Once with the government, I had plans aplenty—all originating in Washington! For my life, from that time until my retirement thirty-seven years later, was given over to frequent change, "by order," with new places to live, new jobs to be performed, new friends, new associates, new foods, new social customs. This book should be a testimony to how interesting a life can be without a plan of one's own making.

At the turn of the century, there were just over 100 commissioned officers, most of whom knew one another and all of whom were known and watched by the Surgeon General. A glimpse of the intimacy of the Service of those days is provided by Grubbs' trip to the American Public Health Association meeting of 1902 from his duty station at Ship Island off the Alabama coast. At the New Orleans meeting, Surgeon General Wyman called Grubbs aside and introduced him to

Mexico's minister of health. Plague, which had first occurred in San Francisco two years before, was now appearing in Mexico. Wyman asked Grubbs to go immediately to Ensenada in Baja California at the invitation of the Mexican government to investigate. Grubbs left for the West the next day, sharing a Pullman compartment with the Surgeon General who was, himself, on his way to Los Angeles. They tossed a coin, according to Grubbs, to see who got the upper berth.

With the American entrance into the First World War, Grubbs was assigned to "cantonment duty" at military facilities in Newport News, Virginia. Working with local physicians and donated supplies, he set up a public health system, built a laboratory, and quarantined infected prostitutes. In 1918, he crossed to France on a troop transport. Lice, venereal disease and submarines, he reported, were the principal hazards encountered by soldiers on the way to the front.

In Grubbs' view, the commission, coming as it did from the president, was essential to the idea of the Service, meaning the officer "must go on order anywhere in the world and stay there until he is ordered to another duty." Branham's experience notwithstanding, Grubbs held that the commission made the position and pay secure for life and therefore warranted the organizational fealty he describes. Grubbs' career included assignments in the marine hospitals and quarantine duty, research at the Hygienic Laboratory and medical diplomacy in Europe, ear, nose and throat training in Germany and troop transport assignments during the Spanish-American War. By his tally, he had twenty-one homes that were considered permanent, with only three of them for as long as four years. Movement was constant. The Service was home.

From 1911 when Leslie Lumsden went to Yakima County, Washington to help stem a typhoid epidemic, rural sanitation campaigns were central to the work of the Service. "Lumsden's boys," as his trainees were called, taught proper waste disposal methods (right) and initiated programs in health education. Once the new privies were built, municipalities collected the full cans at specified intervals and presented the owners with clean, empty ones (below). Ramshackle privies (opposite above) were common. The Service gave its seal of approval to properly designed ones (opposite below).

the Governor of Massachusetts asked that a Service officer, Dr. Allan McLaughlin, be loaned to the state to become its first commissioner of health under a new system enacted by the legislature. McLaughlin served for four years in that capacity, building a regionalized public health system staffed by full-time, trained health officers—a system that was emulated by a number of other states. In later years, an assignment to state government became an important career step for many commissioned officers and built bonds between state and federal public health leaders.

The growth of state and local health departments was tied to an important new element in the developing tapestry of American public health—the rural sanitary campaign. In 1911, Dr. Leslie Lumsden, a Service officer who had distinguished himself for work on typhoid fever, was sent to the state of Washington at the request of Yakima County. His charge was to investigate the source of typhoid fever in the county whose rate was more than three times that of the state as a whole. His simple conclusion was that feces were the problem and that the county should "Abolish every insanitary privy, privy vault, cess pool and septic tank in the city and replace those in the non-sewered areas by sanitary privies."[12]

Not bashful in his recommendations, Lumsden went on to propose the establishment of "an efficient county health organization" to be staffed by full-time, trained personnel. His prescription for typhoid fever produced a dramatic decline in its incidence in the summer of 1911, prompting the Yakima County commissioners and the city council to establish a permanent local health department staffed by a physician, a sanitarian, a nurse and a clerk. This success led the Public Health Service to publish a monograph by Lumsden entitled "The Causation and Prevention of Typhoid Fever—with Special Reference to Conditions Observed in Yakima County Washington." The monograph received wide distribution and became something of a bible for rural sanitation work as well as a blueprint for the development of county health departments. Although public health agencies existed in several counties prior to 1911, the Yakima achievement and Lumsden's leadership led to the subsequent development of county health departments in most parts of the country.

The reformist spirit of the Progressive Movement unwittingly rekindled a controversy that had many elements in common with the Hamilton-Billings dispute. In 1906, a prominent group of Progressives organized the Committee of One Hundred for National Health whose principal aim was the creation of a national department of health. The group assembled under the auspices of the American Association for the Advancement of Science in response to the campaign of two Yale economists, Irving

Fisher and J. Pease Norton. Fisher and Norton advocated conserving human resources to stimulate "national efficiency" and a national department was central to their goals. This department would do all that the Public Health and Marine Hospital Service was doing and more. It would consolidate the food and drugs section of the Department of Agriculture, the Indian Affairs and Territorial Health Services in the Department of the Interior, the medical care of federal prisoners, and the industrial hygiene portion of the Bureau of Mines with the Public Health and Marine Hospital Service in a cabinet level department. The debate was complicated by the emergence of a vocal and motley opposition calling itself the National League for Medical Freedom representing interests as diverse as patent medicine manufacturers and antivivisectionists.

By 1910, some thirteen bills proposing a national health department or changes in the Public Health and Marine Hospital Service were introduced in the Congress. These bills presented a delicate political challenge for the veteran Surgeon General, Wyman, who was not opposed to a department of health but was determined not to be preempted by it. Moreover, his own agenda for Service expansion was far from complete. He especially wanted authority to investigate water pollution and noninfectious diseases, to get the pay and privileges of commissioned officers put on a par with the military, and to obtain authority to commission the Hygienic Laboratory's professors. Ambitious though they were, these goals were largely parochial. Despite Surgeon General Wyman's consistent and largely successful efforts to expand research, quarantine, and disease control programs, his vision remained that of a Marine Hospital Service officer. Illustrative of this was his gruff response to the sponsors of a proposal to establish a Children's Bureau within the Service. Dr. Milton Rosenau described Wyman, the aging bachelor, as being ". . . most emphatic in his refusal to complicate his life with the importunities of a group of sentimental women who were interested solely in the welfare of mothers and infants."[13] Subsequently the Children's Bureau was created in the Department of Labor.

On November 21, 1911, Wyman died suddenly, leaving the variety of proposals for federal health reform unresolved. Wyman's legislative maneuvering had been adroit and, although Progressives were certain he was active in blocking the legislation, he had managed to avoid overt resistance to the health department concept. The Public Health and Marine Hospital Service, to be sure, had been an instrument of Progressive reform during his long tenure. But Wyman's legacy was not a new institution encompassing all of the nation's medical and public health aspirations. Rather it was a corps of skilled, disciplined, health soldiers, caring still for the merchant marine and now combatting infectious disease effectively and specifically. Doctors Woodworth and Hamilton would have approved.

(To Be Tacked Inside of the Privy and NOT Torn Down.)

Sanitary Privies Are Cheaper Than Coffins

For Health's Sake let's keep this Privy CLEAN. Bad privies (and no privies at all) are our greatest cause of Disease. Clean people or families will help us keep this place clean. It should be kept as clean as the house because it spreads more diseases.

The User Must Keep It Clean Inside. Wash the Seat Occasionally

How to Keep a Safe Privy:

1. *Have the back perfectly screened against flies and animals.*
2. *Have a hinged door over the seat and keep it CLOSED when not in use.*
3. *Have a bucket beneath to catch the Excreta.*
4. *VENTILATE THE VAULT.*
5. *See that the privy is kept clean inside and out, or take the blame on yourself if some member of your family dies of Typhoid Fever.*

Some of the Diseases Spread by Filthy Privies:

Typhoid Fever, Bowel Troubles of Children, Dysenteries, Hookworms, Cholera, some Tuberculosis. The Flies that You See in the Privy Will Soon Be in the Dining Room.

Walker County Board of Health

Public Health Warriors

The PHS waged war against disease in the field and in the laboratory. The work was hard, sometimes rewarding and, occasionally, hazardous. Public health campaigning was not always glamorous. The trachoma researcher (opposite) has been brought to a temporary standstill in his quest for cases on an Indian reservation.

Surgeon General Wyman was a well known national figure at the time of his death. "No better recognition of this man," eulogized Treasury Secretary Franklin MacVeagh, "who did so much to build the service up and who was so eager to carry it forward, could be made than to promote and expand its usefulness."[1] In this spirit but with far less sweep than many wanted, the Congress passed a law in August of 1912 that did finally and permanently change the name of the Service to the Public Health Service (PHS). The law did not reorganize federal health activities nor did it allow for the commissioning of non-physician employees of the PHS. Importantly, though, it extended the authority of the Public Health Service to "investigate the diseases of man and conditions influencing the propagation and spread thereof, including sanitation and sewage and the pollution either directly or indirectly of the navigable streams and lakes of the United States." All illnesses of man and his environment were now fair targets for the PHS.

Dr. Rupert Blue was President Taft's surprise choice as the new Surgeon General. Selected over a number of more senior officers, the forty-six-year-old Blue was stationed in Hawaii at the time, serving as an advisor to the territorial health department in its campaign against yellow fever. He had gained acclaim for his eradication of plague from the city of San Francisco following the 1906 earthquake by use of quarantine and rat-trapping techniques and his demonstration of federal leadership in a regional public health emergency.

A quiet man with a handlebar mustache, Blue had been an amateur boxer as a youth. As Surgeon General, he was at ease with visitors of all sorts, cordially receiving the occasional friend from his boxing and rat-trapping days amidst the more usual professional callers. A seasoned practitioner of public health, Blue appointed able deputies from among those with whom he had worked in the field—notably W. Colby Rucker as Assistant Surgeon General and George McCoy who, in 1915, became director of the Hygienic Laboratory. In 1916, Blue was elected president of the American Medical Association (AMA), the only Surgeon General ever to enjoy that distinction. His election came at an extraordinary moment when the leaders of organized medicine and the public health movement both supported the development of local health departments and a system of national health insurance to pay for medical care. "Experience has shown," stated Blue in his presidential address to the AMA,

that an adequate health insurance system should distribute the cost of sickness among those responsible for conditions causing it and thereby lighten the burden on the individual. Financial incentive may thus be given for the inauguration of comprehensive measures for the prevention of disease.[2]

The subsequent involvement of the United States in the First World War preempted these discussions and, after the war, this vision and the organizational unanimity behind it were gone. The health department idea, though, fared better than did the idea of health insurance in the years that followed.

T he Public Health Service Act of 1912 made explicit what had been an increasingly important element of the work of the Service from 1887 when the Hygienic Laboratory opened—the all-out exploration of disease in the laboratory and in the field. The technology of that early research, the actual machinery of science, was rudimentary by later standards. Similarly, the collaborative emphasis of subsequent research where teams of scientists were to investigate human biology, was well in the future. The early PHS scientists were themselves the principal ingredient of the research program. They faced the historic plagues of mankind armed with simple technology and their own cunning. Many contracted the diseases they stalked. Some triumphed and began campaigns of eradication. A few perished.

Yellow fever was among the most destructive and perplexing of 19th century scourges. In 1898, Service physician Henry Rose Carter

Public health work had many manifestations. The new popular emphasis on health and hygiene is evident at the Wilson County Sanitation Day Parade held in Fredonia, Kansas in 1915 (opposite above). The PHS designed and used a special railroad car laboratory (below) to support sanitary campaigns in this same period. Henry Rose Carter (opposite below), a Service officer whose concept of "extrinsic incubation" contributed to Walter Reed's identification of the mosquito as the vector of yellow fever, is seen here collecting insect larvae.

PHS efforts to study the newly-discovered disease, tularemia, included rounding up large numbers of rabbits (below), one of the primary sources of infection. A PHS officer and three rabbit drovers (right) pause during their labors. Dr. Rupert Blue (opposite) served as Surgeon General from 1912 to 1920. Early in his Service career, he gained distinction for leading the campaign that eradicated plague in San Francisco in 1907. Following his two terms as Surgeon General, he remained on duty in the PHS for another twelve years, retiring in 1932.

KANSAS RABBIT DRIVE

carefully plotted the progress of an epidemic of the disease in two small Mississippi towns, concluding that there was an "extrinsic incubation period" between human infections. "The fact that yellow fever is not directly transferable from the sick to the well," Carter wrote, ". . . is held to be due to the fact that the material leaving the person of the patient must undergo, and does undergo, some change in the environment before it is capable of infecting another man."[3] Carter had not identified the mosquito as the intermediate host, but his thesis had an important impact on the Army's Walter Reed who led the team that successfully demonstrated that the *Aedes aegypti* mosquito was the vector of yellow fever. Reed subsequently wrote to Carter saying, "You must not forget that your own work in Mississippi did more to impress me with the importance of an intermediate host than everything else put together."[4]

In 1902, Charles Wardell Stiles, a twenty-six-year-old scientist from the Department of Agriculture became the first director of the Division of Zoology at the Hygienic Laboratory. He was fascinated by a little understood parasite, the North American hookworm, that he had been the first to describe and name. His studies were to demonstrate the staggering level of human infestation in the American South—a quiet pestilence that robbed millions of people of health and productivity and came to be called "the germ of laziness." Despite resistance from a medical profession disinclined to believe in an epidemic they had not diagnosed and the smirking levity of the press ("The Microbe of Sloth" or "Cracker Disease"), Stiles persisted in his efforts to generate concern about hookworm.

Since the Public Health Service had neither the people nor budget to mount the massive assault on rural sanitation that was needed to prevent endemic hookworm disease, Stiles looked for a private patron. In 1908, a fortunate series of events put him in touch with Frederick Gates, John D. Rockefeller's ambassador of philanthropy, and led to the founding of the Rockefeller Sanitary Commission. Rockefeller endowed the Commission with $1 million to combat hookworm with the proviso that the money be spent in five years and be channelled through the health departments of the thirteen southern states. Stiles served as the scientific director of the Commission which, by 1914, had examined more than half a million children in 600 southern counties, finding a 39 percent rate of infection. The campaign focused on privy construction to promote the sanitary disposal of human excreta. Though the topic was often greeted with embarrassment or derision, Stiles labored to build public awareness of hookworm disease and developed innovations such as scoring systems for privies that ranged from 100 for a "Water Carriage or Marine Hospital Barrel" privy to zero for "No Privy at all." Stiles' work set the stage for rural sanitary reform throughout the nation, proved an enormous stimulus to the development of health departments in the South, and

helped shape the agenda of the nascent Rockefeller Foundation— soon to be the world's largest philanthropy.[5]

While Stiles brought the depredations of hookworm to the attention of the public, other diseases were called to the attention of the Public Health Service. In 1902, the State of Montana asked for help with a mysterious ailment called "black measles" that caused illness and death among woodsmen and ranch hands. Over the following decades, the Service assigned a number of scientists and eventually set up a permanent laboratory in Hamilton, Montana, to study the disease which was soon proven to be tick borne and named "Rocky Mountain spotted fever." In 1911, Dr. Thomas McClintic was sent to Montana from the Hygienic Laboratory to set up an experimental control program, dipping livestock and exterminating small animals. As he was completing his work, he contracted the disease. Prompted by a desire to see his wife whom he had married just before leaving for the West, McClintic returned to Washington where he died shortly after his arrival. He was one of eight Americans, five of them affiliated with the PHS, who died as martyrs to the study of Rocky Mountain spotted fever.[6]

The conquest of trachoma, a chronic, debilitating and, ultimately, blinding infection of the eyes, was the chosen cause of John McMullen. A large and affable man reared in the South, McMullen was schooled in trachoma surgery—the only curative treatment at the time—on Ellis Island where he served from 1904 to 1911. McMullen began his twelve-year war on trachoma when he was sent to Kentucky in 1912 to conduct a trachoma survey in response to a request for assistance from the state. The survey showed some 8 percent of the 18,000 people examined to be infected—figures dramatic enough to warrant special language in the 1913 Federal Appropriations Act authorizing the Public Health Service to treat trachoma patients.

In the ensuing years, "Big Doc" McMullen became a familiar figure in the back country of Appalachia from Missouri to West Virginia. "The whole family," he wrote of his patients, "often sleep, live, and cook in the one room of the home . . . .If a disease as contagious as trachoma is introduced, all the facilities for its rapid transmission will be found present."[7] He set up more than a dozen temporary trachoma hospitals staffed by nurses employed by the PHS who cared for convalescing patients and ran personal hygiene and health education campaigns in the surrounding areas. McMullen, often using a mule for transportation, would ride the circuit between the hospitals and outlying clinics, performing surgery assisted by local physicians and preaching the doctrine of soap and water and separate towels. In 1924, "Big Doc" retired from the trachoma war, having led the campaign that controlled the disease well before antibiotics, having himself salvaged the sight of thousands of people.

The most perplexing of the diseases facing the Public Health Ser-

The Carville complex abutting the Mississippi in central Lousiana.

Hansen's Disease . . . and Carville

For thousands of years, Hansen's disease has afflicted the human race and has stigmatized its victims. Traditionally known as leprosy, the disease has been feared everywhere for its prevalence, its presumed contagiousness, and its ability to cause disfigurement and blindness.

Throughout this century, the Public Health Service has engaged in leprosy research and treatment. In 1901, the Marine Hospital Service issued the first national report on leprosy, noting that there were 278 cases but that the count was incomplete because there was "an inclination . . . to conceal the affliction from the public." In 1905, Congress provided the Service with $150,000 for a leprosy hospital and laboratory to be established in Hawaii where the disease was prevalent. On the isolated island at Molokai, the Service designed and built a handsome facility that boasted the first flush toilets in Hawaii. The Hawaiian leprosy venture, however, proved to be a brave failure with patients refusing to submit to the routine of hospital life. The facility had served only nine people when it was closed in 1911.

As early as 1894, a crusading doctor opened a leprosarium in Carville, Louisiana. He smuggled his first patients onto the grounds and claimed to be running an ostrich farm so as not to incense neighboring landowners. In 1917, Congress enacted legislation designating the facility at Carville as the National Leprosarium and charging the PHS with its management. Early treatment at Carville included the application of traditional remedies such as chaulmoogra oil from India to patients but it was the work of PHS researcher, Dr. Guy Faget, which brought real hope

to leprosy patients. In 1941, Faget began using sulfone derivatives in experimental treatment with excellent results. Sulfone therapy revolutionized leprosy therapy at Carville and elsewhere and enabled many long term patients to leave the institution.

Today Carville has 130 residents, most of whom are elderly. Although there are only 6,000 cases in the United States, it is estimated that 15 million people worldwide suffer from leprosy making it one of the world's great, continuing epidemics. Research at what is now called the National Hansen's Disease Center has been enhanced by the discovery that the armadillo is susceptible to leprosy, providing the first known host other than man for the study of the disease. This research focuses on identifying new agents to prevent and treat leprosy as well as the development of limb-sparing therapies and devices—a technology that has important applications for diabetes and other degenerative diseases in addition to Hansen's Disease.

Dr. Waldemar Kirchheimer and an armadillo used in leprosy research.

vice in this period was pellagra, a scaly, red, skin eruption that progressed through stages of cramps, diarrhea, dementia, and death. Known for 200 years in Europe, it had never been reported in this country before 1906 but was rampant by 1912, especially in the South and among poor and institutionalized populations. The 1913 Appropriations Act that set McMullen to work on trachoma also funded a PHS hospital for pellagra research at Spartansburg, South Carolina. Surgeon General Blue chose Dr. Joseph Goldberger to direct the pellagra effort. Goldberger, born in Hungary, had grown up delivering groceries on New York's lower east side, graduated from Bellevue, and was a fifteen-year veteran of contagious disease research who had distinguished himself in field studies of typhus fever and yellow fever. From the outset he doubted the prevalent view that pellagra was an infectious disease. His observation that institutional populations suffered from the disease while the staffs of the same institutions did not, led him to the first speculation that diet might cause pellagra.

By June of 1914, he was confident enough to announce his theory that it was a dietary deficiency of milk, meat, and eggs that lay at the root of the disease but he needed further proof. Twelve healthy, convict volunteers at a Mississippi state prison agreed to eat a high carbohydrate diet devoid of milk, meat, and fruit. Within six months, five of the group had developed the symptoms of pellagra leading Goldberger to conclude in 1915 that "Pellagra is not a communicable (neither infectious nor contagious) disease, but that it is essentially dietary in origin . . . (and) that no pellagra develops in those who consume a mixed, well-balanced and varied diet."[8] Skeptics remained, and for them Goldberger conducted his most dramatic experiments, feeding pills made from the skin and bodily discharges of pellagrins to

Montana's Bitterroot Valley (above) was the site of an illness called "black measles" by local residents, which came to be known as Rocky Mountain spotted fever. Starting in 1902, the PHS sent scientists to the area who eventually identified ticks as the agent of disease transmission and, subsequently, staffed a permanent laboratory in Victor, Montana. Animals such as the mountain goat (opposite) were found to serve as hosts for the ticks.

volunteers in his laboratory and to himself—with no ill effects. For a final touch, he injected his wife with the blood of a woman with pellagra. She too remained in good health.

Working with the assistance of Edgar Sydenstricker, a brilliant young PHS statistician, Goldberger did extensive studies on the social epidemiology of pellagra and documented its close relationship to the economy. He also identified brewers yeast as a simple, inexpensive preventive agent, although it was not until 1937, eight years after Goldberger's death, that nicotinic acid was identified as the specific vitamin deficiency underlying pellagra. Of all the Public Health Service field scientists, Goldberger is, perhaps, the best known because of his singleness of purpose and the spectacular success his work achieved in thwarting pellagra.[9]

The advent of the First World War created significant and unexpected dilemmas for the Public Health Service. The achievements of the Service in controlling disease and caring for merchant seamen were indisputable and well known, but its identity as a national institution was challenged by the entrance of the United States into the First World War in April of 1917. The military draft that followed presented both symbolic and practical issues for the Service.

Although an Executive Order issued by President Wilson on April 3, 1917, made the Public Health Service a part of the military forces of the United States, the role of the PHS in the international

Vaccination against Rocky Mountain spotted fever took place without regard for location, as this rancher (below) discovered. PHS bacteriologist Ida Bengston (opposite), working in a sterile room at the Hygienic Laboratory, prepares tissue cultures for work on Rocky Mountain spotted fever.

70

Under the direction of Dr. John "Big Doc" McMullen, (opposite above left, in white coat) the Public Health Service, working with state and local health departments, carried out a fifteen-year campaign against trachoma in Appalachia. The only treatment for severe cases was surgical debridement of the eyelids, which was often performed in temporary clinics set up in schools and meeting halls (opposite below). The equipment was then packed up and carried to the next location. The PHS also conducted laboratory studies of trachoma (opposite above right).

conflict was uncertain. Some officers were detailed to the Army and the Navy. Others sought to resign their commissions in order to join the military forces. A resolution of the Mutual Benevolent Association of the Public Health Service in November of that year called on the Surgeon General to transfer the Service in its entirety to the Army or the Navy for the duration of the war. The lone dissenter on the committee drafting the resolution was Leslie Lumsden, the builder of health departments and privies. Pugnaciously, he argued for the integrity and mission of the Service:

> If the work of the Public Health Service as a public health service with its remarkable spirit of team work manifested in its fights against epidemics of yellow fever and bubonic plague and against insanitary conditions in our vast rural districts ever were needed that time is now. It seems, therefore, that . . . we should endeavor . . . to have the Service strengthened . . . so that we may do well the great war work which is ours to do.[10]

The proposal went forward to President Wilson at a Cabinet meeting at which Treasury Secretary William McAdoo, to whom the PHS reported, was absent. The President referred the proposal to McAdoo who settled the issue by flatly rejecting the transfer idea and thereby maintaining the integrity of the PHS.

It was the military draft, though, that defined the principal war work of the PHS. By the fall of 1917, half a million men had been conscripted and sent to hastily constructed training camps—a figure that would reach three million by the war's end. These cantonment areas became instant public health hazards, having little in the way of sanitation and creating conditions ripe for the outbreak of diseases such as malaria and typhoid fever. Working with the Red Cross and local health officials in circumstances that were often chaotic and always poorly funded, the PHS set to work constructing public health systems around military posts, targeting mosquitos, human excreta, impure water, and venereal disease.

Samuel Grubbs was one of many PHS officers assigned to cantonment work, and was given responsibility for several military installations in Virginia's Newport News area. Working with local physicians and businessmen, a $21,000 grant from the Red Cross, and fifty trucks donated by Henry Ford, Grubbs designed and managed a rigorous disease control system for the area. Venereal disease proved to be his toughest problem requiring political and social as well as medical skills. A previously recalcitrant local judge agreed to back Grubbs' aggressive campaign, stating that although he was "not in favor of prosecuting anybody for breaking the Seventh Commandment, whether they do it for pay or not," he was persuaded that "if we can quarantine for yellow fever, we should be able to lock a woman up who may spread gonorrhea."[11] Grubbs, backed by the judge, established a system of testing, contact tracing, and isolation, and built a small hospital facility where infected prostitutes were housed and treated.

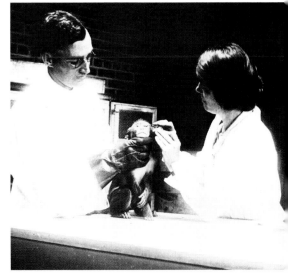

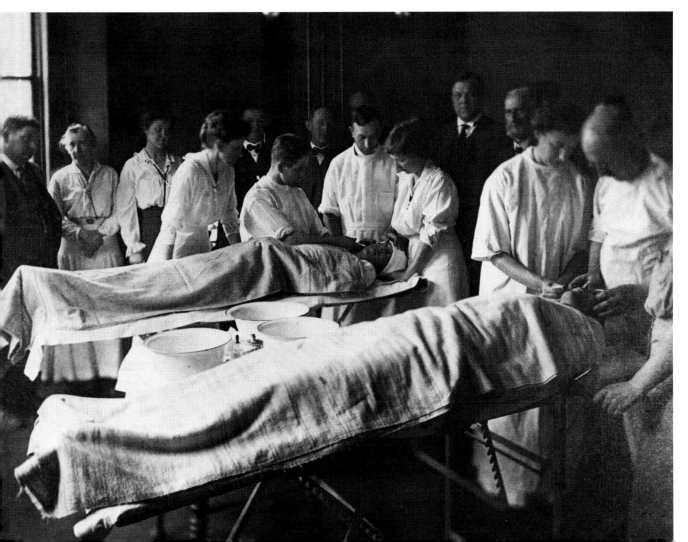

Indeed, the war focused attention on venereal disease. The cumulative impact of prostitution, military encampments, and the debilitating effect of venereal infection on the war effort brought a new public frankness to bear on the long standing problem of venereal disease. "Soldiers are not prisoners," wrote Grubbs.

> They must be allowed recreation these last few days on native soil. They do not want to be told to be good, hence if we did not protect them outside the camps and assure them clean companions, infection would strike them down more surely than the enemy bullets.[12]

The Army Appropriation Act of 1918 established a PHS Division of Venereal Diseases with a $2 million budget and a mandate to work through state health departments to control the spread of "social disease." Although the funds for veneral disease control plummeted after the war ended, the perceived menace to American troops initiated and legitimatized PHS venereal disease work—an area of research and control activity that has continued to the present.

As American involvement in the war reached its height in the summer of 1918, a severe respiratory illness dubbed "Spanish flu" surfaced in Europe. In September, flu cases appeared in New England and spread rapidly across the country. Public health officials realized that an epidemic was at hand. On October 1, 1918, Congress passed a resolution directing "the Public Health Service to combat and suppress the 'Spanish influenza'" and appropriating $1 million for the battle. In the ensuing months, sixty-four commissioned officers—almost one third of the Corps—were assigned to flu work and more than 2,000 doctors, nurses, and clerks were hired by the PHS for in-

In the first decade of the 20th century, pellagra emerged as a prevalent disease in the American South—particularly in institutional settings. Most scientists assumed it to be an infectious disease but Joseph Goldberger (opposite above), assigned by the PHS to investigate pellagra, did not. His work at the Pellagra Hospital (below) in Spartansburg, South Carolina, and elsewhere in the South demonstrated that dietary factors were responsible for causing and curing the disease. In Goldberger's pellagra research laboratory (opposite below), various diets were prepared and fed to volunteers. Goldberger used his research associates, his wife, and himself, as well as prisoner volunteers, as experimental subjects.

fluenza duty. The disease was everywhere. Dr. Alice Evans, a scientist at the Hygienic Laboratory, described dropping her research on meningococci to begin work on flu, only to find herself feeling ill. "I put away my utensils and ingredients and went home. A little more than a month later I returned to work."[13] By December, the epidemic had begun to subside, to be followed by a second wave in the spring of 1919. In all, the flu struck five million Americans, leaving 500,000 of them dead.

The war quickly created veterans—millions of veterans—who had a special claim on the nation as a consequence of their service to the country. Legislation in 1917 set up the War Risk Insurance Bureau and called on the Marine Hospital system to provide care for disabled soldiers. The law was augmented in 1919 charging the PHS with responsibility for the care of all returning veterans. To do this, the Service was given a small budget increase and the authority to appoint reserve officers to augment its ranks and to acquire existing federal buildings. Growth took place in a rapid and often unsatisfactory manner, with barracks and training camp facilities as well as old military hospitals being pressed into service for the care of veterans. By 1921, the PHS' Division of Hospitals was running sixty-two institutions (only twenty of which were originally Marine Hospitals) and had registered an eight-fold increase in the number of patients treated over the pre-war level.[14]

The system was so overloaded that even the staid, PHS *Annual Report* complained gently in 1920 that "The Public Health Service

During the First World War, the Public Health Service in cooperation with local health departments was responsible for keeping the areas around military training camps (called extracantonment zones) free from disease (above left). PHS officers worked to persuade local citizens (left) of the value of keeping their property clean. Oil dripped into streams from specially contrived cans (above) was a principal method used to control mosquitos and, thereby, malaria. The boys being given typhoid inoculations (right below) were part of a PHS rural sanitary program. Note the priest in the car recording the proceedings.

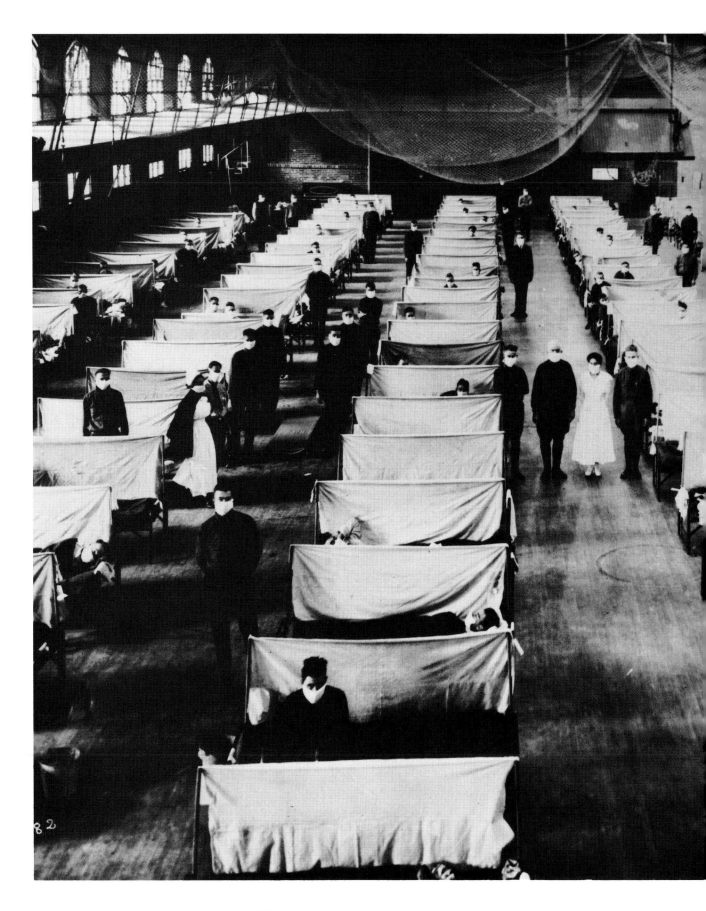

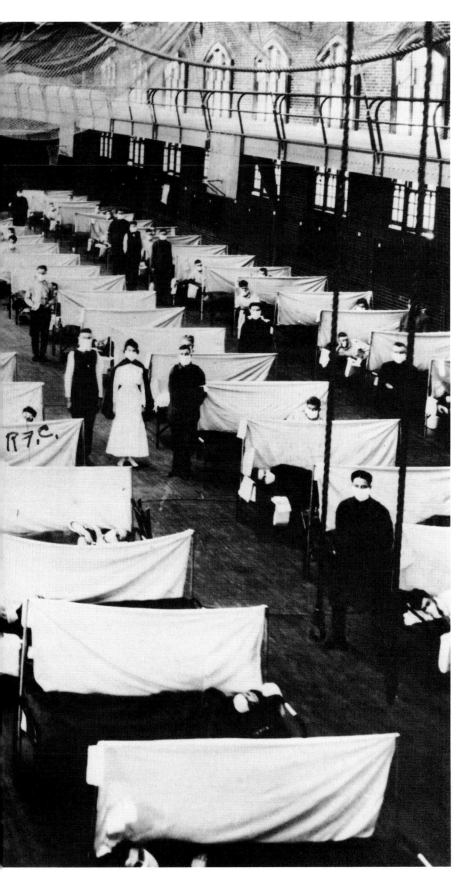

INFLUENZA
FREQUENTLY COMPLICATED WITH
PNEUMONIA
IS PREVALENT AT THIS TIME THROUGHOUT AMERICA.
THIS THEATRE IS CO-OPERATING WITH THE DEPARTMENT OF HEALTH.
YOU MUST DO THE SAME
IF YOU HAVE A COLD AND ARE COUGHING AND
SNEEZING. DO NOT ENTER THIS THEATRE
GO HOME AND GO TO BED UNTIL YOU ARE WELL.

Coughing, Sneezing or Spitting Will Not Be
Permitted In The Theatre. In case you
must cough or Sneeze, do so in your own hand-
kerchief, and if the Coughing or Sneezing
Persists Leave The Theatre At Once.

This Theatre has agreed to co-operate with
the Department Of Health in disseminating
the truth about Influenza, and thus serve
a great educational purpose.

**HELP US TO KEEP CHICAGO THE
HEALTHIEST CITY IN THE WORLD**
JOHN DILL ROBERTSON
COMMISSIONER OF HEALTH

*In 1918 and 1919, Spanish flu attacked
some five million Americans and left
half-a-million people dead in its wake.
Congress voted the PHS a $1 million
appropriation to hire doctors and nurses
to care for the sick. One-third of the
Commissioned Corps was diverted to flu
duty during this period. The epidemic
defeated public health measures
employed to protect against it although
workers at massive infirmaries, such as
this one at the Iowa State University
gymnasium (left), took what precautions
they could. Public health officials tried
to instruct as many people as possible
about the dangers of influenza. In Chicago, theater operators were required to
exhibit precautionary posters (above).*

felt, and still feels, that it would be wise for the National Government to undertake the construction of proper hospital facilities for the care of ex-servicemen and women."[15] Pushed by a strong movement among veterans' organizations, Congress established an independent Veterans' Bureau which, in April of 1922, took over 57 hospitals with 17,000 beds leaving the PHS with 24 Marine Hospitals with 3,000 beds. The PHS survived the separation although the size of its budget, swollen as it was with appropriations for veterans' care, fell sharply in 1923. Successfully, if unwittingly, the PHS had given birth to the Veterans Bureau (now the Department of Veterans Affairs) hospital system.

War had brought uncertainty to the Public Health Service, challenging its role and durability. Yet the PHS had come away from the war intact, neither having been absorbed by the military nor overwhelmed by the veterans' movement. Moreover, the period between Dr. Wyman's death and the departure of the Veterans Bureau had seen major changes in the nature of the PHS. Not only were new diseases being challenged, but the composition of the Service began to change as it grew. Nurses, in particular, became a central part of PHS programs, staffing Ellis Island, the trachoma clinics, the PHS Pellagra Hospital, and the Marine Hospitals. During the war, PHS nurses participated in extra-cantonment and venereal disease work and served in the hospitals caring for veterans. In 1919, Surgeon General Blue appointed Lucy Minnegerode, previously of the Red Cross, as PHS Superintendent of Nurses.

As was the case with all health professionals except physicians, nurses were employed as civil servants. In 1918, under the duress of the war, Congress did pass legislation allowing dentists, pharmacists, and sanitary engineers to be commissioned as reserve officers, but many PHS health professionals and all technical staff, including the large number of support personnel necessary to run the hospitals, were civil service employees. In 1915, for example, of 2,131 PHS staff, only 187 were commissioned officers. A decade later after the Veterans Bureau had come and gone, there were 182 regular service officers and 68 reserve officers among the 4,672 PHS employees.[16] Although the Commissioned Corps continued to provide the leadership, the PHS had become a far larger and broader institution than was the all male, Marine Hospital, physician cadre that had spawned it half a century earlier.

The First World War was a watershed in public health as it was in national life in general. With the election of Warren Harding in 1920, the electorate embraced "not nostrums, but normalcy" and effectively repudiated two decades of aggressive public solutions to the problems of community life. Progressivism and the sanitary reform movement were now part of history. New science lay ahead in the decade to come but so did an entirely new political environment.

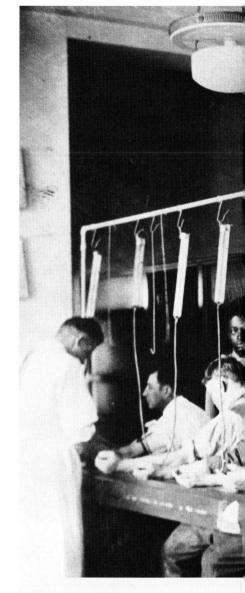

Surgeon Sage Says—

Only a poor boob pays his money, loses his watch, gets the syph, and brags that he's had a good time.

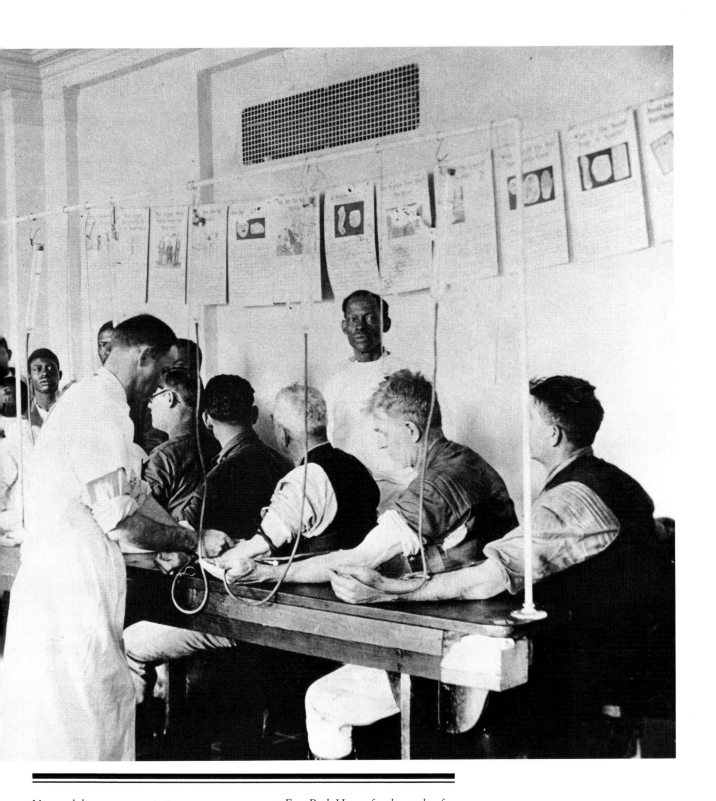

Venereal disease was an important theme in the research, prevention, and treatment programs of the Public Health Service from the time of the First World War. In Hot Springs, Arkansas, the PHS ran a clinic (above) at the Government Free Bath House for the study of venereal disease. During the war, posters (left) were an important part of the campaign to keep the troops free of venereal disease and fit to fight.

Public Health Within Limits

On March 10, 1920, President Wilson appointed Hugh S. Cumming to succeed Rupert Blue as Surgeon General. Conservative, aristocratic in bearing, and politically adroit, Cumming was the quintessential commissioned officer of his epoch. A University of Virginia Medical School graduate, he joined the Service in 1892 and worked at the Staten Island Marine Hospital, on plague control in San Francisco, and quarantine duty in Georgia. He served four years in Japan and was representing the PHS in Europe at the time of his appointment. Cumming brought to the office of Surgeon General a sophistication but also a philosophy different from his predecessors—a strategic complacency that left much public health authority with states and communities and that, the *New York Times* reported, had "little sympathy for those who would transfer this responsibility to Washington."[1]

This philosophy was consistent with a postwar nation bent on "normalcy," dedicated to big business, and generally inclined to see poverty as the result of personal failure. It was not, however, always consistent with the continued developments in medical and sanitary science and with the evolving public health problems of the country. Necessity, experience, and curiosity led to the constant expansion of the definition of public health as practiced by the PHS. Paradoxically, Cumming's very conservatism combined with his political agility and his long tenure allowed for growth in the size and concept of the PHS that might not have been possible under less canny leadership.

Two critical elements in the future of public health were pioneered by the PHS in these years—epidemiology and biostatistics. As early as 1913, Dr. Wade Hampton Frost, aided by a team of medical officers, sanitary engineers, and bacteriologists, moved into a ramshackle, former marine hospital in Cincinnati and began the nation's first systematic studies of water quality and pollution. Working closely with scientists at the Hygienic Laboratory, they analyzed the waters of the Ohio River. This was followed in later years by studies of many of the nation's waterways including the Mississippi and Illinois Rivers and Lake Michigan. In 1919, Frost was detailed to the new Johns Hopkins School of Hygiene and Public Health as its first professor of epidemiology whence he continued to run the Cincinnati laboratory. Not only did these studies allow Frost and his colleagues to apply epidemiological techniques to the relationship between water supplies and disease, but the subsequent work of these scientists on sewage

treatment and water purification marked the inception of the discipline of environmental health science.

Biostatistics was the domain of Edgar Sydenstricker, a young man trained in economics who became the Service's first statistician when he joined the PHS in 1915. He demonstrated both his extraordinary abilities and the utility of statistics in his studies with Goldberger on pellagra and his work with Frost during the 1918 flu epidemic. He developed the techniques of intensive door-to-door data collection—now known as the household survey—and began an extended study of the population of Washington County, Maryland, which he and Frost transformed into a scientific art form that still flourishes today. In 1921, he became chief of the Office of Statistical Investigations with a staff of clerks which, the *Annual Report* of 1922 proudly reported, had "counting, sorting, tabulating, cardpunching, computing, calculating, and graphing machines and devices." Under Sydenstricker's guidance, the PHS entered the age of statistics.

Two poorly understood and socially uncomfortable issues that inexorably entered the domain of the PHS were "mental hygiene" and drug addiction. Ellis Island presented the examining officers with constant challenges as to what was normal behavior and what was not and, as early as 1914, Dr. Lawrence Kolb had initiated studies of mental health and alcohol and drug addiction among arriving immigrants. "The public has again demanded that the physician shall extend his field of activity—that he shall become acquainted with the field of mental deficiency," wrote an officer of the growing PHS interest in behavioral problems. "The physician will be called on to decide as to whether a given individual will be committed to a home for the feeble-minded or to some other institution for the sick."[2] The staffing of Veterans Bureau psychiatric hospitals by the PHS gave Kolb and others growing expertise in these poorly mapped areas. Narcotics addiction became a public concern following newspaper accounts of drugs in Hollywood and led to demands for a better understanding of addiction. Although the care of the mentally ill remained a responsibility of the states, research on these problems fell to PHS investigators who, working at the Hygienic Laboratory and travelling abroad, labored to gain a better understanding of the workings of the mind.

In 1929, Congress enacted legislation that established a Narcotics Division (subsequently renamed the Division of Mental Hygiene) within the Public Health Service and mandated the construction of two facilities to treat and study addicts. The first of these "narcotics farms" was opened in 1935 at Lexington, Kentucky with the seasoned Dr. Kolb as its director. Although the majority of patients were federal prisoners necessitating a secure facility, the treatment philosophy of Kolb and his collaborator, Dr. Walter Treadway, was withdrawal and rehabilitation. The Lexington hospital was located on a 1,000 acre working farm, designed and staffed as an educational and vocational

The presence, quality, and management of water was an active concern of the PHS from the early years of this century. PHS scientists began monitoring water quality and methods of purification in streams, lakes, and rivers (opposite above) following an Act of 1912 that assigned the Service this responsibility. The battle against yellow fever included public education in proper water storage and drainage techniques as well as inspection of property (opposite below right). Sanitary engineer J.A. LePrince (opposite below left) inspects standing water for evidence of mosquito larvae in the campaign against yellow fever in Texas in 1924.

Dr. Hugh Cumming's tenure (1920 to 1936) has proved to be the longest of any Surgeon General (opposite above left). A conservative Virginian, he supported expanded research activities but was opposed to increased federal support for state and local health programs. Since the early years of this century, the PHS has been involved in the compilation and interpretation of statistics relating to health and disease. A woman in the Service's Statistical Office (opposite above right) works an adding machine in this 1926 photograph. The card-sorter (opposite below) preceded the computer in the Statistical Office.

training facility. The second PHS narcotics farm was opened in 1938 in Fort Worth, Texas.

In spite of the precipitous decline in congressional support for venereal disease control after the end of the First World War, the PHS maintained its Division of Venereal Diseases, focusing on inexpensive sex education campaigns. In 1926, Dr. Thomas Parran, a physician fresh from state health work in the Midwest who had been recruited to the Service during medical school at a chance meeting with Joseph Kinyoun, took over the division. Parran rekindled working relationships with states and explored various mechanisms for increasing research on and treatment of venereal diseases. He identified syphilis among blacks in the South as a particularly severe problem but the absence of federal funds for treatment programs and the meager state health department budgets made progress virtually impossible.

In 1930, however, the Rosenwald Fund, a private philanthropy committed to the welfare of American blacks, approached the PHS about a collaborative program to study the epidemiology and methods of syphilis treatment in the black South. Although the Fund later dropped out, their backing along with that of numerous state and county health departments helped the PHS launch a modest campaign against syphilis. "We held our clinics usually in the front yard of a church out in the pine woods or next to a turpentine camp," recalled a PHS physician of his assignment to a mobile syphilis unit called a "Bad Blood Wagon" in Brunswick, Georgia.

> On Sundays we'd go to the black churches, take the trailer, pull up to the front door of the church. . . . We'd go in, listen to the preacher preach. . . . At the end of the preaching and singing and the collection, he would lead them all and go right out the front door into the trailer. They'd all get blood tests and they'd come back in. . . . We heard some marvelous singing.[3]

A new Venereal Disease Act in 1935 greatly augmented the funding for the programs and increased the involvement of PHS personnel. In Macon County, Alabama, one of the sites supported by the Rosenwald Fund and subsequently by the Tuskegee Institute, a research project begun in 1930 would continue for four decades before ending amid national controversy. Nonetheless, the attack on syphilis launched by the PHS in this period, dependent as it was on the cumbersome and minimally effective therapies of the pre-antibiotic era, was determined and conscientious.[4]

The opportunities and risks of rewriting the laws that governed the Public Health Service were never far from the desk of the Surgeon General. The expanded areas of PHS activity as well as growing health programs in other agencies of the federal government created a familiar scenario of internal and external pressures for change. In 1921 and again in 1924, Cum-

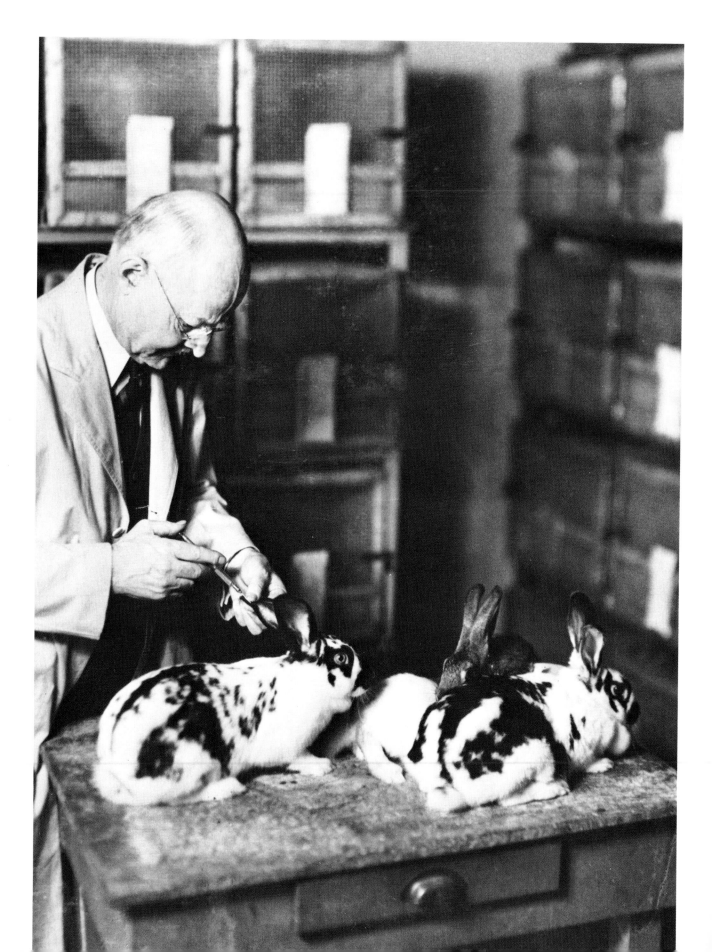

ming tried unsuccessfully to get legislation passed that would allow the commissioning of dentists, scientists, and sanitary engineers in the regular corps and would create a nurse corps. Although Commissioned Corps benefits were better than those of the Civil Service, they were less than those of the military services, leading to several failed efforts to achieve parity in pay with the Army and Navy.

Plans to restructure the Service erupted regularly, starting in 1921 when Utah Senator Reed Smoot proposed permanently consolidating the PHS with the Veterans Bureau and an array of educational and welfare agencies. Smoot was an avowed opponent of the Service, claiming it was abusing the prerogatives of states and communities and intended to "Russianize" the United States. This proposal died but interest in reorganization emerged again in the mid-1920s from an alliance of voluntary organizations called the National Health Council whose analysts showed that, in 1926, 40 different government agencies, located in 5 cabinet departments, employing 5,000 workers carried on public health work.[5] Their answer, once again, was the consolidation of health activities under the leadership of an assistant secretary for public health. Cumming, predictably, did not like the idea and, as Wyman had done before him, parried with a more moderate set of reforms that were embodied in a bill introduced by New York Congressman James S. Parker in 1926. Coordination instead of consolidation was the essence of this proposal with the PHS being given the authority to detail its officers to agencies of the government that needed public health leadership.

These debates were complicated by growing support for a major expansion of the Hygienic Laboratory in size and in concept. As early as 1921, the Chemical Foundation, an organization dedicated to the promotion of chemistry in the United States, published and distributed a million copies of a report entitled *The Future Independence and Progress of American Medicine in the Age of Chemistry* that called for the establishment of a research institute that would systematically apply the fruits of chemistry and physics to the problems of disease and health. The idea flourished, borne aloft by the "can-do" environment of the 1920s. If Henry Ford could bring amazing production efficiency to the factory, surely the same could be done for the scientific laboratory. Private funding, however, did not materialize, and in 1926, Joseph Ransdell of Louisiana, the Senate's senior member and a long time advocate of public health, introduced a bill to create a National Institute of Health (NIH) within the PHS to supplant and expand the Hygienic Laboratory. "Research service," editorialized the *New York Times* in support of the bill,

in the conservation of the health of the nation should not be left entirely to private interest. . . . Particularly it is desirable that chemistry should be brought back, in its highest development as a science, to the aid of the physician in the prevention of disease and the alleviation of suffering.[6]

In 1930, the Ransdell Act transformed the Hygienic Laboratory into the National Institute of Health, acknowledging the progress and promise of biomedical research. NIH scientist Edward Francis (opposite) was noted for his work on tularemia. Often called "the first American disease," all aspects of tularemia were elucidated by PHS researchers including George McCoy, Francis, and Rose Parrott, an NIH investigator who died from a laboratory-acquired tularemia infection. Dr. Herald Rea Cox (below), is shown preparing vaccines. Typhoid was also an early subject of research at NIH (above).

For the next four years the Parker and Ransdell bills were introduced and reintroduced, being amended, combined, separated, passed, and vetoed. Finally, in the spring of 1930, within a month of one another, both were passed and signed by President Hoover. The Parker Act strengthened the Public Health Service in the ways sought by Surgeons General Wyman and Cumming while giving little ground to other departments of government or the proponents of public health reorganization. It provided for regular corps commissions for dentists, pharmacists, sanitary engineers, and Hygienic Laboratory scientists at the level of division director. It gave the Surgeon General latitude in assigning personnel to other agencies and tied the pay of all commissioned officers to that of the Army. The Ransdell Act created a National Institute of Health in the place of the Hygienic Laboratory, appropriated $750,000 for physical expansion, and established a fellowship and private endowment program. Taken together, the two acts gave further substance to the notion of a Public Health Service equipped to move against disease in the laboratory and in the field. The Ransdell Act, in particular, putting in place a formal government research institute with license to explore human health and disease, would help shape the future of science throughout the world.

The freewheeling, business-first life of the nation began a long decline with the stock market crash in October of 1929. Four million Americans were unemployed a year later, seven million by the fall of 1931 and eleven million by late in 1932. Businesses failed, banks closed, mortgages were foreclosed, and farmers left the land. Steadfast in their principles, the Hoover administration opposed government intervention, believing that the economy would bottom out and the basic mercantile soundness of the country would reassert itself. The president cleaved to the policy that relief was a matter for local government assisted by private charity, an impossibility for many communities which were ill equipped to deal with the epidemic of poverty raging in their midst.

Within the ranks of the Public Health Service, there were varying attitudes about what role the Service should play vis-a-vis local government in the developing crisis. There was, of course, a strong tradition of technical assistance provided by the PHS to state and local health departments. Leslie Lumsden had made a career of spawning county health departments; by 1928 there were 204 of them in 17 states. Working out of his command post at the Hygienic Laboratory, he had trained a generation of public health workers (many of whom identified themselves fondly and proudly as "Lumsden's boys") in rural sanitary work and health department advocacy.

Cumming had a far more detached view of the proper PHS role in local health matters as evinced by his opposition to the Sheppard-

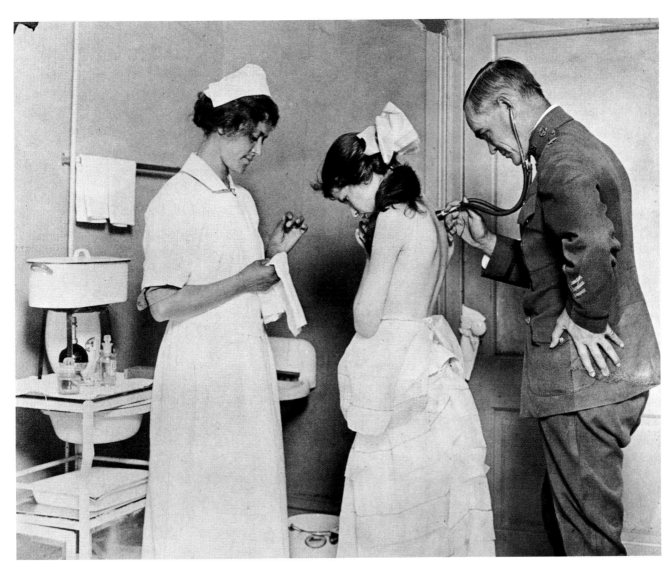

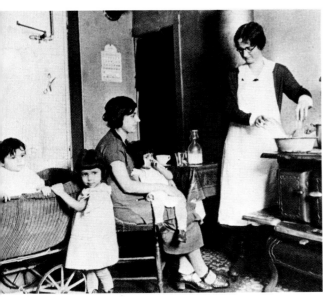

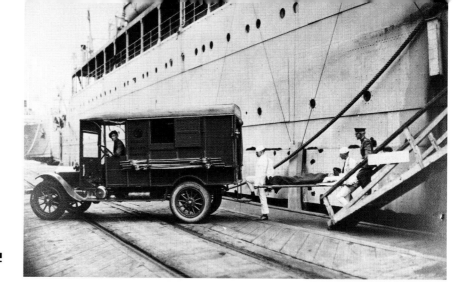

The Marine Hospitals remained at the heart of the PHS enterprise during this period, employing the majority of PHS personnel and serving as a training ground for physicians, dentists and other clinicians joining the PHS. An ambulance (above left) from the Norfolk Marine Hospital picks up a patient at the dock in 1923. The camaraderie of shared experience and hospitals they could call their own meant a great deal to American sailors. Hospitalized seamen (right) pose in 1920 with a model ship memento of their maritime calling, and relax in the lounge of the New Orleans Hospital in the 1930s (above right). The most landlocked Marine Hospital was the facility at Ft. Stanton, New Mexico. A former Army fort in the Indian Wars, the PHS ran it as a tuberculosis sanitarium. The photo of the tent (above center) was captioned, "A consumptive on Easy Street."

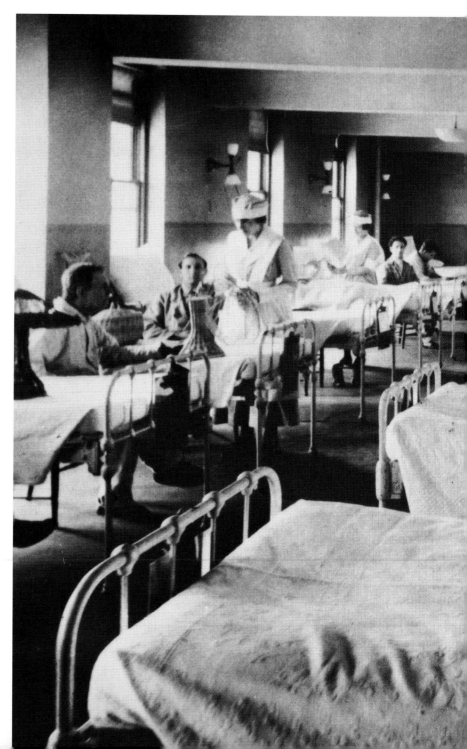

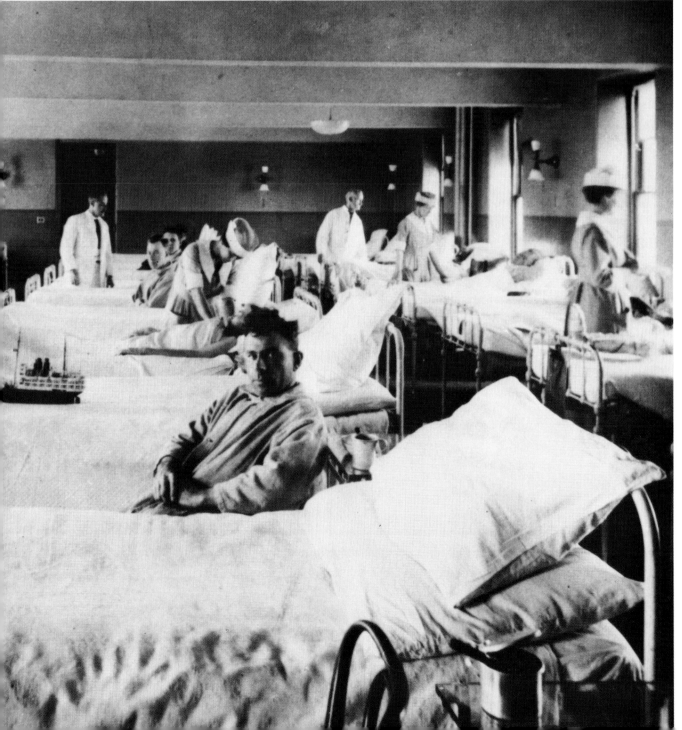

Towner Maternity and Infancy Act. This 1921 legislation provided federal grants to states to teach prenatal and infant care to mothers and was administered by the Children's Bureau, supervised by a board which included the Surgeon General. Uncomfortable with state grants and opposed to their management outside of the PHS, Cumming joined with the American Medical Association in successful opposition to renewal of the legislation in 1929.

The quiet rivalry between Cumming and Lumsden that had existed since 1920 when the latter had been a candidate for the job of Surgeon General was exacerbated by the Depression. Lumsden, with congressional backing, wanted increased PHS funding for county health services and sought to make the support permanent rather than "demonstration." Cumming disagreed. Late in 1930, Cumming relieved Lumsden of his rural sanitation post and dispatched him to New Orleans to be the largely ceremonial PHS regional director. "Politics about public health and the federal role in health was controversial," recalled Dr. W. Palmer Dearing, then a young PHS officer.

He (Lumsden) was working for a federal role in public health, lobbying for it, if you will. Cumming wanted to be president of the AMA and the AMA was against it. That's the story from Lumsden. That's what he told me. So they invented a job . . . to get him out of town. . . . Lumsden wasn't about to sit in the Customs House in New Orleans and pick his nose. . . . He was detailed to some place over in Texas . . . to inspect the inventory of surplus property of one automobile tire. So in

A mariner leaves the hospital (opposite). In addition to American and foreign seamen, beneficiaries of Marine Hospitals have included members of the military, the Coast Guard, the National Oceanographic and Atmospheric Administration, and seamen of the Mississippi River Commission. The dental clinic at the New Orleans Marine Hospital is shown below as it looked in the mid 1930s. Dental care had long been a part of the services offered in the marine hospitals. Dentists were commissioned into the Reserve Corps in 1919 and into the Regular Corps in 1930.

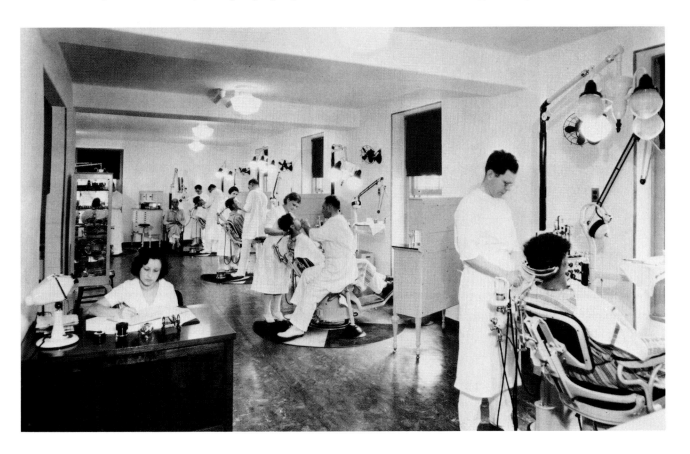

A scene from the La Tuna, Texas Federal Prison showing a PHS physician with a patient and inmate-interpreter.

The Medical Center for Federal Prisoners in Springfield, Missouri shortly after completion in 1933.

The Care of Federal Prisoners

In 1930, President Hoover signed a law creating the Federal Bureau of Prisons (BOP) in the Department of Justice and charged it with developing an integrated correctional system from the 7 federal prisons with 12,000 inmates that then existed. The law also included provisions for the assignment of Public Health Service officers to federal prisons to supervise and provide psychiatric, medical, and other scientific services. Since that time, the PHS has staffed the BOP medical facilities.

Early assignees included physicians, psychiatrists, dentists, nurses, and engineers. The PHS staff was welcomed by prison personnel, with the first BOP director stating that his organization had scored "a ten-strike" when it gained the services and expertise of the PHS.

Officers were put to work at prison hospitals and dispensaries and, after it opened in 1933, the Medical Center for Federal Prisoners in Springfield, Missouri. The latter facility, a 1,200 bed hospital, was built to meet the needs of inmates from around the country who were chronically ill or in need of specialized medical or psychiatric services.

Over the years, the federal prison system has grown, as has the number of PHS officers assigned to it. Today, there are 50,000 inmates in 55 facilities, which include 6 regional hospital centers and a second federal medical center in Rochester, Minnesota that opened in 1985. Approximately 170 PHS officers are on duty with the BOP, continuing the tradition of the provision of care to federal prisoners.

The Depression reduced the standard of living of most citizens and pushed many into poverty. The son of a sharecropper in New Madrid County, Missouri (above) tries to make the best of his world. The need for services was great among the poor, the dispossessed, and migrants (right) from the Dust Bowl.

his formal report, he said he wrote out that he cut up the tire crosswise into strips, two inches across, to be used as hinges for the seat covers (of privies).[7]

Cumming did, indeed, run twice for the presidency of the AMA, narrowly losing in 1934. Lumsden, automobile tires notwithstanding, made good use of his "exile," catalyzing public health screening and health education programs in a number of southern states, building a model for the Social Security health programs of later years.

If Lumsden was the backbone of PHS local health programs, Joseph Mountin was to become its brain. A veteran of cantonment work who spent much of his first years in the Service on assignment with health departments in Missouri and Tennessee, Mountin counted himself one of "Lumsden's boys." From his varied experience running disease control campaigns and working in state and local health administration, he developed a scholarly interest in applied public health. In 1931, he returned to Washington to run a new Office of Public Health Methods for the PHS, applying scientific principles to the study of health department management and practice. Over the next several years, he examined and wrote about a series of timely problems including the relationship of housing to health, accident prevention, and air pollution. Then, as later, he was a believer in the importance of local health departments, stating that "Every Commissioned Officer in the PHS should be required to serve as a local health officer to see at least one budget through the board of supervisors."[8]

Mountin's work began to push at the walls of the traditional definition of public health. Were the limits of health department programs to be population-based, preventive activities or did public health have an additional concern with the actual care rendered in communities? "Let me suggest," he told a gathering of state officials,

> that you turn your attention to the medical services which the community is prepared to render—both the preventive and the curative. Generally speaking this personal aspect of public health protection—services to individuals—has been developed to a far lesser degree than has the environment control. . . . Today social thinking has developed to the point where the nation seems disposed to extend the benefits of medical science to persons needing care for conditions other than tuberculosis and mental disorders.[9]

Mountin's thinking had moved a step beyond Lumsden's. Not only should health departments exist and be supported, but they could be candidates to provide personal health care where none existed. Although public dispensaries for the treatment of the sick poor had existed in many cities from the late 19th century through the Progressive era, these "medical soup kitchens" tended to focus on the education of medical students and young physicians. They were not to be the precursors of a government sponsored medical care. In Mountin's idea, however, resided the kernel of a much larger concept—that of the government as the provider of health care to the general populace. Indeed, the role of the government in regard to medical care

Although venereal disease remained a difficult problem socially and medically, the PHS collaborated with local health departments in sponsoring testing and treatment programs. The mobile clinic (below) called a "bad blood wagon" made the rounds of towns in the vicinity of Brunswick, Georgia. The project was staffed by two local nurses and a young PHS officer and future Surgeon General, Leroy Burney (left). Visiting on this occasion was the then Surgeon General, Thomas Parran (right). The woman (above) is reading a flyer promoting blood testing. Urban campaigns to control syphilis gained some measure of popular support, as is demonstrated by the crowd gathered in Chicago (opposite).

would prove to be an energizing, polarizing and consistent issue for the PHS from the early 1930s on.

This polarizing issue was joined formally by the Committee on the Costs of Medical Care (CCMC)—a blue-ribbon panel that met from 1927 to 1932, supported by a consortium of foundations and agencies including the PHS. Staffed by I. S. Falk, a young microbiologist on leave from the University of Chicago and based at the Hygienic Laboratory, and Edgar Sydenstricker, among others, the CCMC produced a report entitled *Medical Care for the American People* that recommended voluntary health insurance, group medical practice, and government grants for the care of indigent patients. A minority report supported by organized medicine and presaging many battles to come, took issue with these conclusions and favored private, fee-for-service solutions to the problems of medical care.

In the 1920s and the early 1930s, the PHS grew slowly. The marine hospitals remained at the center of the system with new facilities being built and opened in Baltimore, Galveston, New Orleans, Seattle, and Staten Island during this period. The 25 hospitals continued to be the largest employer in a PHS work force that expanded from 4,700 in 1925 to 6,300 a decade later, with the number of commissioned officers increasing from 250 to 400 in the same period. In 1932, Dr. Estella Ford Warner was appointed as an Assistant Surgeon, the first woman commissioned in the Service.

A young physician named Leroy Burney received his commission in 1932 following a year as an intern at the Chicago Marine Hospital and a year studying public health at Johns Hopkins. His five days of written and clinical examinations were followed by an interview with the board during which he was called on to discuss "characters from Dickens" and the Indian tribes of his native state, Indiana. "It was very pleasant but still firm," he recalls. His first assignment was to the Cleveland Marine Hospital where he rotated between medical and surgical duties and lived with his wife in quarters on the grounds that "were beautifully furnished with a grandfather clock, linens, silver and so forth." During that first year, though, Burney spent a month's furlough back in Indiana because he, like everyone else in the PHS, was required to take thirty days of unpaid leave to relieve the federal budget at the height of the Depression.[10]

Burney then spent five months at the PHS clinic in Hot Springs, Arkansas learning about venereal disease and its treatment, followed by a year as the venereal disease specialist at the Hudson-Jay clinic in New York, another as a medical officer at the Medical Center for Federal Prisoners in Springfield, Missouri, and then a reassignment to Chicago. Typical for young officers, the frequency of these moves and the type of assignments limited the usual comforts of a settled life and a familiar community. Service protocol—prescribed formalities between commissioned officers—helped ease the awkwardness of fre-

Malaria continued to be an important public health concern and was a particular hazard to people living in the rural areas of the South (opposite above left). During the Depression the PHS sponsored programs aimed at malaria control that in later years included aerial spraying of mosquito larvicides (opposite below). PHS officer J.E. Dent (opposite above right) uses "Paris green-lime" mixture to spray water-filled tires that served as a mosquito breeding ground in Charleston, South Carolina.

quent resettlement for PHS personnel and their families. Newly assigned officers, for instance, as well as those departing were directed to call on their superiors who, in turn, were to provide them with hospitality. Calling cards were to be left when families were not at home with "p.p.c." (pour prendre conge . . . to say good-bye) marked on the cards of those slated to leave. "Social calls, dances, dinner parties, luncheons, teas and receptions took the edge off all-too-grim reality," writes Susan Volkmar, the daughter and granddaughter of Service Officers, "and made some semblance of 'normal living' possible. The intricacies of protocol afforded some privacy to those thrown into close association by the exigencies of work."[11]

The effects of the Depression on health added urgency to the debate on the role of public health, yet the PHS was given little new to work with during the Hoover administration. With the election of Roosevelt in 1932 and the advent of the New Deal, the PHS became part of the broad strategy to get the national economy moving again. In collaboration with other agencies of the new administration, programs were mounted for malaria control in the South, rat control in seaports, the sealing of abandoned mines to prevent stream pollution and, presumably, to what must have been Lumsden's delight, the construction of $5 million worth of rural privies. The Rocky Mountain Laboratory produced quantities of spotted fever vaccine for the Civilian Conservation Corps. Between October of 1935 and March of 1936, the PHS conducted a National Health Survey designed to document the incidence of chronic disease and disability in the population. The survey demonstrated the relationship between health and poverty, showing that disabling illness was 57 percent higher and chronic illness 87 percent more prevalent among families on relief than among those with adequate incomes.[12]

It was, however, the Social Security Act of 1935 that would provide the PHS with the mandate to become an important, independent participant in the reconstruction of the country. That Act and, indeed, the New Deal as a whole invited PHS involvement in the medical and social fabric of the country in a more intense way than ever before. Grants-in-aid to states, counties, and cities, the political battles over national health insurance, and the measurement of the health of communities were to become principal issues for the PHS. These issues would all place stress on the older and less controversial definition of the PHS that remained based in the Marine Hospitals. As the politics of health gradually and permanently climbed onto the national agenda, the boundaries of the PHS would be the subject of continued debate. Was the PHS simply the institutionalized heir of the hygienic reform movement of earlier years, or was it the proxy and, perhaps, future national department of health?

Chapter Five
1936-1948

Calamity, Necessity, and Opportunity

"I think we have reached a stage in our civilization when we must accept as a major premise that citizens should have an equal opportunity for health as an inherent right with the right of liberty and the pursuit of happiness."

Surgeon General Thomas Parran, 1937

The Cadet Nurse Corps was established during the Second World War and funded through the PHS in order to meet the increased need for nurses caused by the war. Recruiting posters such as this one (opposite) glamorized the nurse and appealed to young women's feelings of patriotism.

The Depression was a calamity for the nation and, like the war that followed, it called forth vast and unforeseen changes in American social and political life. Its punishing effects on all elements of the nation and the tenacity with which it continued well into the 1930s created a political environment in which extremist ideas and personalities on both the right and left flourished. The New Deal as crafted by President Roosevelt and his partisans aimed down the middle, offending radicals frequently and business consistently, but avoiding the twin sirens of communism and fascism that beckoned persistently. It was the experiment, the large-scale political and social improvisation—the Tennessee Valley Authority, the Civilian Conservation Corps, the Works Progress Administration—that characterized the New Deal more than adherence to any specific ideology.

The Social Security Act of 1935 was a good example of New Deal pragmatism. Although the law included three of the key elements of social insurance—old age benefits, unemployment coverage, and workers' compensation—it did not include sickness insurance. Strategic and vociferous opposition by organized medicine as well as Depression-spurred support for the balance of the program prompted Roosevelt to move ahead without health insurance. Even without these provisions, the Social Security Act represented landmark health legislation. Title V of the Act reestablished a program of grants to states for maternal and child health services, administered by the Children's Bureau, breathing life back into the concept underlying the Sheppard-Towner law, and initiated child welfare and crippled children's programs. Title VI was a springboard for the PHS. It provided the Service with the funds and the authority to build a system of state and local health departments—an activity it had been doing informally since Leslie Lumsden paid his visit to Yakima County in the summer of 1911.

It was no accident that Title VI was well suited to the mission of the PHS. The legislation had been proposed by members of the president's Science Advisory Board including the New York state health commissioner, Dr. Thomas Parran. A commissioned officer and a former head of the Venereal Disease Division, Parran had been detailed by the PHS to the state of New York in 1930 at the request of the governor, Franklin Roosevelt. In the spring of 1936, at the end of Surgeon General Cumming's fourth term, President Roosevelt

104

Under the terms of the Social Security Act passed in 1935, the PHS provided funds and technical assistance to state and local health departments to support such community health activities as visiting nurse programs (above). PHS officers also worked with the Farm Security Administration in setting up rural medical cooperatives that helped to pay the medical bills of farm families hard pressed by the Depression.

brought Parran back to Washington, appointing him Surgeon General. Parran's view of public health was considerably broader than that of his predecessors, having an activist quality to it that smacked of the New Deal. "For a long time," he had stated in 1934, "statesmen have expressed the thought that the care of the public health is a primary responsibility of government. . . . So far, however, the performance of such services is more theory than fact. Public health has not been a major issue of our Government in the past."[1]

Armed with the Social Security Act, Parran went to work making public health a major issue of government throughout the country. Title VI provided for grants to states that were based on a formula that included population, financial need, and the existence of special health problems. It required state matching funds to stimulate the development of comprehensive programs of state and local public health services that would be aided by the federal government but run at the state and local level. It also provided money to train public health workers and to undertake research on public health problems. This was Lumsden's vision writ large. This was, at last, the formal and funded opportunity for the PHS to serve as mentor, partner, and counsellor to the health departments of the nation.

During the final months of 1936, the PHS received plans from every state for the development of public health systems under the provisions of the Social Security Act, and the program of state grants began in earnest. PHS support for industrial hygiene and plague control was added to the malaria control, privy construction, and mine-sealing activities already underway. The PHS made consultation services available to local health departments in nutrition, dental hygiene, laboratory methods, and accounting, and the Division of Domestic Quarantine that housed these programs eventually became the Division of State Relations.

Venereal disease was an area of particular concern to Parran. In 1934, while he was still the New York State health commissioner, CBS had cancelled his appearance on a scheduled national radio broadcast because he refused to delete the word "syphilis" from his text, resulting in a flurry of national print news stories that netted "syphilis" a great deal of attention. His 1937 book, *Shadow on the Land,* treated sexually transmitted diseases explicitly and thoroughly and contributed to a growing atmosphere of scientific frankness in regard to venereal disease. The Lafayette-Bulwinkle Act of 1938 provided the PHS with a major appropriation to augment venereal disease control programs through grants to state and local health departments. These control efforts were revolutionized by the work of Dr. John Mahoney of the Venereal Disease Research Laboratory at the Staten Island Marine Hospital, who, in 1937, demonstrated the effectiveness of sulfa drugs in treating gonorrhea, and six years later proved the utility of penicillin in combatting syphilis.

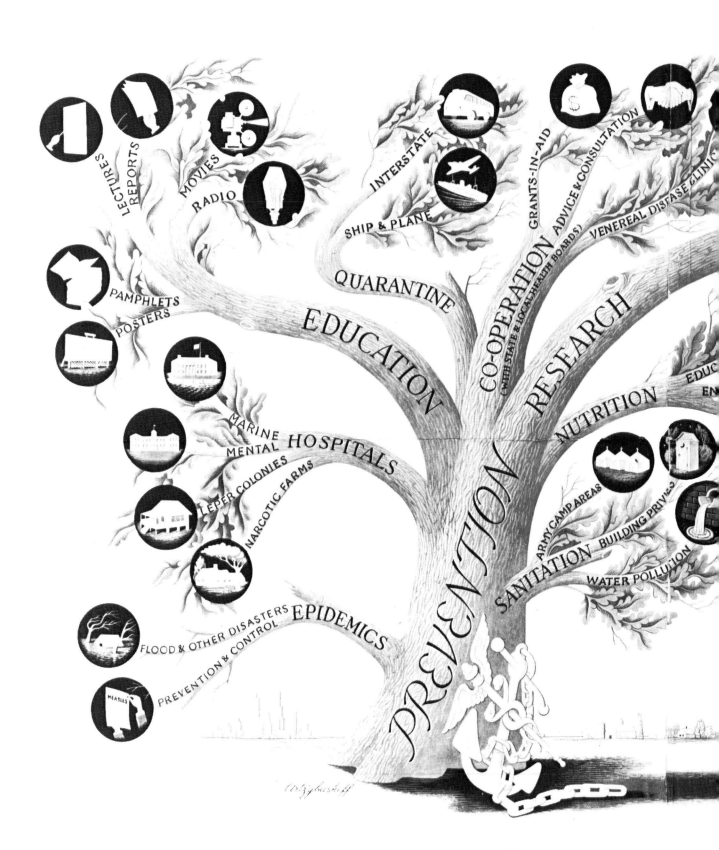

LECTURES
REPORTS
MOVIES
RADIO
PAMPHLETS
POSTERS
MARINE
MENTAL HOSPITALS
LEPER COLONIES
NARCOTIC FARMS
FLOOD & OTHER DISASTERS
EPIDEMICS
PREVENTION & CONTROL
MEASLES
QUARANTINE
INTERSTATE
SHIP & PLANE
EDUCATION
CO-OPERATION
(WITH STATE & LOCAL HEALTH BOARDS)
GRANTS-IN-AID
ADVICE & CONSULTATION
VENEREAL DISEASE CLINIC
RESEARCH
NUTRITION
EDUC
EN
SANITATION
ARMY CAMP AREAS
BUILDING PRIVIES
WATER POLLUTION
PREVENTION

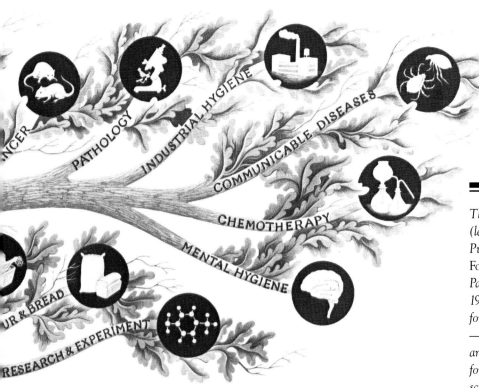

This drawing of a public health "tree" (left) depicting the varied tasks of the Public Health Service appeared in Fortune *magazine in 1941. Thomas Parran (below), Surgeon General from 1936 to 1948, was an ardent publicist for the public health causes of his time —most notably venereal disease—and an advocate of expanded responsibilities for the PHS in medical care and scientific research.*

Although sickness insurance was not a part of the Social Security program as enacted, the issue of medical care remained alive for the country and for the PHS. In what the *Saturday Evening Post* called "a gigantic rehearsal for health insurance," the Service worked with the Farm Security Administration in organizing rural medical cooperatives to help impoverished farm families obtain medical care.[2] On a policy level, the PHS served with the Social Security Board, the Children's Bureau, and the Departments of Interior and Agriculture on the Interdepartmental Committee for Health and Welfare Activities which drafted recommendations for a "National Health Plan." The plan called for significant expansion of public health and maternal and child health services as well as consideration of "a general medical care program supported by taxes, insurance, or both."[3] This report, based in large part on the findings of the National Health Survey, led to a National Health Conference convened in Washington in 1938 that was attended by representatives of labor, farmers, and the health professions. The conference endorsed the Interdepartmental Committee's recommendations over the objections of the AMA.

In 1939, Senator Robert Wagner of New York introduced a bill drawn from the conference recommendations that failed to pass but reemerged in 1943 as the Wagner-Murray-Dingell Bill. In various forms, this proposal served as the battleground for health insurance proponents and opponents through the end of the 1940s when the

TAKING **VD** HOME TOO, SAILOR?

FURLOUGH "Booby Trap!"

NO is the best tactic; the next, PROphylactic!

growth of voluntary health insurance and political conservatism finally combined to kill it. Although I. S. Falk was the principal architect of the National Health Plan on which the legislation was based, Joseph Mountin and PHS statistician George St. John Perrott, supported by Parran, had worked closely with him. Thus the continuing debate on medical care put the AMA and the PHS at odds with one another. Parran, for example, never served as the PHS delegate to the AMA in contrast to his predecessor, Hugh Cumming, who had run for its presidency.[4] Nonetheless, the conservatism of some within the PHS, as well as its many connections with the medical profession, placed the Service at odds with its allies in the government. "This was a battle between Public Health and Social Security," W. Palmer Dearing recalled about the many interagency debates.

> Public Health had to get along somehow with the physicians. But then we were seen as the enemy by the go-go folks at the Children's Bureau and Social Security. We were the enemy because we didn't go for everything they wanted.[5]

The ongoing question of the allegiance of the PHS to the idea of health insurance and the preemption of the issue by others in government—particularly the "go-go folks" at Social Security— would have important effects on the PHS in later years when medical care for the elderly and the poor became overriding public concerns.

In the short term, relations with the Social Security Board became more important for the PHS. In 1939, Roosevelt did what politicians, Surgeons General, and health constituents of all persuasions had argued about since the days of the National Board of Health. He reorganized. Using the authority that allowed the president to rearrange agencies in the absence of specific congressional disapproval, he aligned the Public Health Service with the Civilian Conservation Corps, the National Youth Administration, the Office of Education, the United States Employment Service, and the Social Security Board in the newly created Federal Security Agency (FSA). Subsequent additions to the FSA included the Food and Drug Administra-

tion (FDA), St. Elizabeths Hospital and Freedmen's Hospital, the Children's Bureau, and the National Office of Vital Statistics, rounding out what would become the Department of Health, Education, and Welfare (HEW) in 1953. Although the design of the FSA had elements in common with the reorganizational schemes of health advocates of previous years, it constituted more of a reform in governmental housekeeping than it did a redefinition of the federal role in health. The leadership, style, and work of the PHS was relatively unaffected by its new affiliation.[6]

Medical research grew in stature and viability during these years. Senator Joseph Ransdell had given birth to an important new concept with the passage of the act creating the NIH in 1930. Initially the new law meant little more than a name change for the old Hygienic Laboratory, given the scarcity of government funds and the traditional vision of Surgeon General Cumming and longtime laboratory director, George McCoy. Parran and Lewis R. Thompson, the director of the Division of Scientific Research, envisioned a greatly expanded national medical research program and saw the NIH at the center of it. Serendipity helped them when, in 1935, Mr. and Mrs. Luke I. Wilson offered their forty-five-acre estate in suburban Bethesda to the government and Parran, drawing on his relationship with the president, argued successfully that it should be designated as the new site of the NIH. Parran, who grasped the enormous potential of the spacious campus for the future growth of biomedical research, replaced McCoy with Thompson as the NIH director in 1937, and oversaw the opening of the first buildings at the new location in 1938.

By stages, the NIH had begun to shift the emphasis of its research toward diseases that were less acute and often noninfectious in nature. In part, this was the result of the success of previous work defining and controlling the contagious ailments and, in part, it was due to the growing prominence of illnesses such as cancer and heart disease in a population that was living longer. The National Cancer Act of 1937, passed unanimously by the House and Senate, established the National Cancer Institute (NCI) and inaugurated the categorical approach to NIH research where funds and facilities were dedicated to a single disease. The legislation also provided for a new and, in the eyes of some, controversial experiment—an extramural grant program for the support of cancer investigators at institutions other than the NIH. In many ways, the National Cancer Institute foreshadowed the future, initiating, as it did, not only the categorical approach and the extramural system, but presaging the increasing emphasis on chronic disease research that was to become the core of the powerful NIH apparatus of later years.

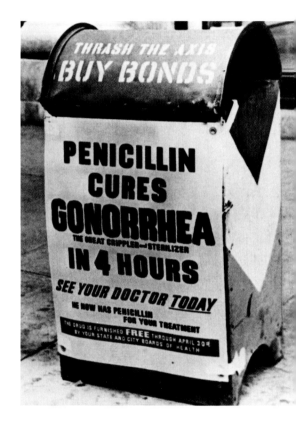

"Mickey" (opposite right) solicited soldiers near a training camp in the southern United States during the Second World War. As part of its venereal disease control activities, the PHS ran special camps to treat infected prostitutes. Posters (opposite above and below) played a prominent role in the program to prevent venereal disease and encourage its treatment.

One of the most successful research adventures of the PHS began not at the NIH but in Naples, Italy in 1901. John Eager, a Marine Hospital Service physician assigned to international quarantine duty in Naples reported an odd finding to Surgeon General Walter Wyman. Numbers of emigrants who came from areas surrounding Naples had severely blackened teeth that were "apparently strong and serviceable." His observation was published in *Public Health Reports* about the same time that a young dentist named Frederick McKay reported a similar phenomenon in Colorado Springs, Colorado. McKay persisted for the next thirty years in his exploration of the syndrome of stained and mottled but otherwise healthy teeth that occurred in widely scattered communities around the United States.

McKay kindled the interest of Grover A. Kempf, director of Child Hygiene Investigations for the PHS. In 1928, McKay and Kempf visited Bauxite, Arkansas, a town owned by the Aluminum Company of America in which virtually every child had stained teeth. An analysis of the Bauxite water revealed a strikingly elevated level of fluoride. The new National Institute of Health took on the mottled teeth problem, appointing H. Trendley Dean as its first dental research scientist. Dean, one of the original dentists commissioned in the PHS, was a ten-year veteran of the Marine Hospital system when he joined the NIH staff in 1931 and set about a systematic analysis of communities plagued by mottled teeth. In 1933, he concluded that elevated fluoride levels in the water supply caused discoloration of teeth but also conferred protection against dental caries—tooth decay.

Dean assembled a team of applied and basic scientists at the NIH to investigate the epidemiology of "endemic fluorosis" and the relationship of fluoride to human metabolism. If safe levels of fluoride could be established, the possibility of eliminating dental caries—a truly epidemic disease—lay before them. At the outset of the Second World War, 400,000 potential recruits—more than 10 percent of those examined—were rejected because they lacked the six opposing teeth the military required to "bite the cartridge." Twice during the war dental standards were lowered and military dentists conducted massive programs of dental restoration. Carious teeth were part of the American way of life.

By 1945, the dental research group had sufficient evidence on dose and safety to attempt a community-wide trial of water fluoridation. The city of Grand Rapids, Michigan volunteered to be the site of the first population-based experiment, with the neighboring city of Muskegon serving as the comparison community. The fifteen-year study involved annual dental exams for all the school children in both towns. By 1950, the inhibition of tooth decay was so dramatic in the Grand Rapids children that the PHS was able to pronounce fluoridation to be safe and effective and the town of Muskegon aban-

doned the experiment in favor of fluoridation. Meanwhile, Congress acted in 1948 to establish the National Institute of Dental Research (NIDR) at the NIH, making dental studies a permanent part of the growing federal research enterprise. Trendley Dean became the new institute's first director.[7]

With the approach of the Second World War, the programs of the PHS began to emphasize military preparedness. A PHS officer was assigned to the office of the surgeon in each of the nine Army Service Commands and charged with overseeing food inspection, sewage disposal, and venereal disease and tuberculosis control. The Surgeon General went to Great Britain to study wartime health problems and the management of civil defense. When United States involvement in the war began, five PHS medical officers stationed in the Philippines were among the first prisoners taken by the Japanese. Two of these physicians eventually died in captivity.

The degree of disruption of civil and industrial life in the United States that the war might cause was unknown, but the experience in Great Britain suggested that it would be severe. In May of 1941, the president established an Office of Civilian Defense and appointed New York Mayor Fiorello LaGuardia as its director. LaGuardia chose George Baehr, an internist who was a member of the New York State Public Health Council, as his chief medical officer. In the belief that the country should have "one national health service, and not two or three competing," Baehr, with Palmer Dearing as his deputy, developed the medical component of the Office of Civilian Defense within the PHS, using reserve corps appointments to bring many senior people into the Service.[8] Medical and engineering officers were assigned to Civilian Defense Regions to coordinate the development of state emergency medical service plans and implement a nationwide system of more than 300 casualty-receiving hospitals.

When, in November of 1941, the U.S. Coast Guard was militarized, the PHS went to war as well. From 1941 to 1945, 663 medical, dental, engineer, and nurse officers served with the Coast Guard, many of them sustaining injuries and four of them losing their lives. Coast Guard ships saw extensive action providing North Atlantic convoy protection, troop support in the Mediterranean and Pacific, and coastal patrols at home. The larger vessels were staffed by PHS physicians who often worked under harrowing conditions patching together the survivors of mine explosions or torpedo attacks. The records of the Coast Guard Cutter *Comanche* for February 3, 1943, for instance, report PHS physician I. Ray Howard laboring "in an improvised hospital ward on a tossing ship pursued by German submarines" treating the survivors of the torpedoed transport ship, *Dorchester*.[9]

During the Second World War, the PHS continued to provide medical care to the Coast Guard. PHS physician James Todd (opposite), based on a Coast Guard destroyer escort, uses a boatswain's chair to reach an injured sailor on a merchant ship in the Mediterranean in 1943. Eight PHS officers died in the line of duty during the war. Among many other duties on the home front, the PHS trained food handlers in the sanitary preparation and serving of food. "Four-fingered Annie" (above) demonstrates how not to carry clean glasses.

Dr. Ralph Braund was the chief of a PHS team staffing the U.S.S. *Bayfield* during the D-Day invasion in June of 1944. "We stayed off the coast from the 6th to the 26th," he wrote to a PHS colleague,

acting as a hospital ship for those casualties brought from the beach and from ships sunk in the area. The number we had aboard at one time varied as we sent them back to England when they could be moved. Our high was 312 on one day. For sixty hours in one stretch the boys were on duty. I drank so much coffee that I was having extra systoles every 4th or 5th beat.[10]

The log of the Coast Guard Cutter *Forsyth* recorded that on May 15, 1945, PHS physician Ralph B. Samson performed a "major operation" at sea on an American sailor who had been wounded by a pistol while boarding a German U-boat. Samson, the log noted, was assisted by the German U-boat doctor who volunteered to help save the American sailor's life.[11]

Numbers of PHS officers were detailed to the military services during the war. Dr. Victor Haas led a team of fifteen PHS physicians, sanitary engineers, and pharmacists assigned to the Army in the China-Burma-India theater of war. The unit was in charge of public health for 150,000 workers building a railroad from China to Burma between 1941 and 1943. A number of Service officers, including Leonard Scheele, trained in military government at the University of Virginia and were detailed to the Army in Europe. Scheele served in Britain at Supreme Headquarters Allied Expeditionary Forces before assignments in North Africa, Italy, and Germany, moving forward with the advancing armies and taking charge of public health in liberated areas. The PHS provided large numbers of clinicians and public health administrators to the United Nations Relief and Rehabilitation Administration (UNRRA) to staff disease prevention and medical care programs in refugee camps in Europe and the Middle East. These assignments increased as the war wound down.

During the war, NIH research was slanted heavily toward studies relevant to military concerns such as the development of synthetic substitutes for opium and quinine. A crash program conducted in close coordination with the Army and the Navy succeeded in producing a vaccine against endemic typhus. By the war's end, the United States had inoculated all of its troops, and several million doses were distributed to civilians through UNRRA.[12] Hematologic researchers developed a pyrogenicity test after whole blood and plasma were found to produce fever in some recipients. The current system of attaching an extra container to a unit of blood came about as a result of the discovery that donated blood could be contaminated when samples were removed for testing purposes.[13] By the latter part of the war, the PHS working in conjunction with the Office of Scientific Research and Development, had expanded its grants and contracts to university researchers in what would become the NIH extramural program of the postwar era.[14]

Maritime Roots— The PHS and the Coast Guard

When Congress created the Marine Hospital Service in 1798 and placed it in the Treasury Department's Revenue Marine Division, it was the beginning of a 190-year relationship between the two agencies dedicated to American maritime life. The successors of those programs today are the United States Public Health Service and the United States Coast Guard.

Starting in 1799, sailors in the United States Revenue Marine Service were assessed dues of twenty cents per month—as were American merchant seamen—in return for which they were eligible for services at marine hospitals. Throughout the history of the Revenue Marine Service—which was renamed the Revenue-Cutter Service in 1863, and merged with the Life-Saving Service in 1915 to become the Coast Guard—marine hospital benefits continued. Light-House Service personnel, subsumed by the Coast Guard in 1938, also received care, and by 1950, an average of 300 Coast Guard patients were being treated each day in PHS hospitals and clinics. This coverage was provided until the PHS hospital system was closed in 1981.

Public Health Service involvement with the Coast Guard has not been limited to clinical settings. During the 19th and early 20th century, Marine Hospital Service officers maintained medicine chests at each Life-Saving Service station and beginning in 1920, the PHS broadcast medical advice to ships at sea in cooperation with the Coast Guard. Additionally, PHS medical and dental officers have been assigned to the Coast Guard Academy to provide clinical care since 1906 and

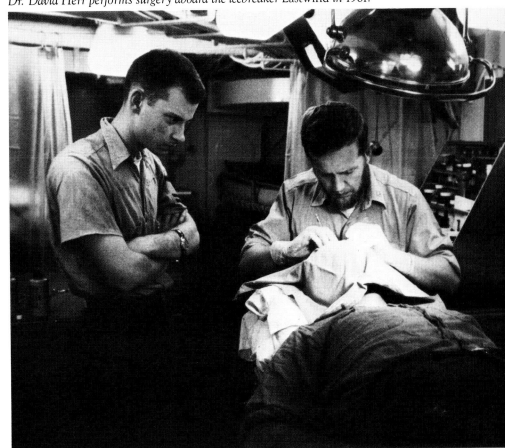

Dr. David Herr performs surgery aboard the icebreaker Eastwind *in 1961.*

1925, respectively. Dental officers provided a special service during the late 1930s when two specially designed mobile dental clinics travelled the country offering services to Coast Guardsmen working at isolated duty stations. The program's slogan was "Be true to your teeth or they may be false to you."

Since the early days of the Service, the PHS has gone to sea with the Coast Guard, providing a medical presence on ships such as the cutter *Bear* which made annual expeditions to the Arctic between 1886 and 1925. Public Health Service officers served with the Coast Guard in combat in the First World War and in the shipping lanes of the Atlantic, Mediterranean and Pacific during the Second World War. Some 660 medical, dental, nurse, and engineer officers were assigned to the Coast Guard in the latter conflict, staffing ships on submarine patrol and providing support for amphibious landings. Three PHS officers were killed in action and, for their work during the war, PHS personnel assigned to the Coast Guard won five purple hearts and three bronze stars.

Despite the closure of the marine hospitals in 1981, the PHS continues to serve with the Coast Guard. Today, there are 160 PHS officers on assignment, including a senior physician who serves as the Chief Medical Officer of the Coast Guard and who holds the rank of Assistant Surgeon General. Public Health Service officers continue to staff Coast Guard missions, participating at times in search and rescue activities. In 1985, a PHS physician lost his life in a helicopter crash near Kodiak Island, Alaska. Public Health Service personnel serve at Coast Guard air stations, bases, support centers, training facilities, and the Academy as well as at sea, carrying on work begun by their predecessors almost 200 years ago.

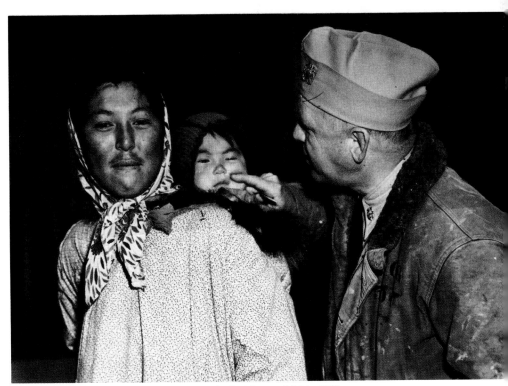

PHS dentist Willis Taylor examines an Alaska Native child in 1951.

Of all the changes in American society wrought by the Second World War, few were as sweeping or as permanent as the entrance of women into the work force. The massive labor requirements of the war industries occurring, as they did, at the very moment that much of the nation's male work force entered military service, left a void filled rapidly and effectively by American women. Nursing presented a particular problem. The chronic national shortage of nurses became much worse as the war progressed, and the nursing needs of the military increased drastically. Nursing faced stiff competition from industrial jobs whose salaries lured both potential recruits as well as established nurses away from the bedside and onto the factory floor.

In consultation with nursing and defense agency leadership, the PHS determined that in 1943, 65,000 women, 10 percent of all high school graduates that year, would need to be recruited into nursing and that a new approach—initially called the "Victory Nurse Corps"—should be tried. This innovative idea quickly gained backers, and the Nurse Training Act of 1943 was passed, creating a $65 million program called the U.S. Cadet Nurse Corps.

Key to recruitment into the Cadet Nurse Corps was an identification with the war effort symbolized by a smart uniform sporting the PHS logo on the beret. Full-tuition scholarships for all participants with a fifteen-dollar-a-month stipend and the promise of "an education for life" provided incentive. Cadet nurses enrolled in approved programs throughout the country, making a commitment to two years of assigned service following their training. The PHS, in turn, underwrote nursing schools through tuition and support payments, training grants, and additional funds to build classrooms and dormitories. Parran created the Division of Nurse Education to run the program and appointed Lucile Petry Leone as its director—the first woman to head a PHS division. The Cadet Nurse Corps was rapidly adopted by the nation, receiving $13 million of donated publicity and technical assistance in its first year. A fashion show to choose the uniform was held at the Waldorf-Astoria and Cadet Corps nurses appeared on billboards and radio spots, newsreels, and magazine covers. The recruitment target of 65,000 was easily exceeded for 1943 as were the goals of the subsequent two years.

With the war over, admission into the Cadet Nurse Corps was terminated and by 1949 the last student had graduated. The program had trained 124,000 nurses with 85 percent of the nursing schools in the country participating. The impact of the Cadet Nurse Corps spread far beyond its original mission of providing staff for hospital wards. From the outset, the program recruited and trained black nurses. Twenty-one black nursing schools participated, as did thirty-eight schools with integrated classes, training a total of 3,000 black nurses. The educational standards developed and enforced by the

During the Second World War, assisted by the introduction of DDT, the PHS resumed its role keeping the areas around military training camps free from malaria (left). The program for Malaria Control in War Areas (MCWA) was based in Atlanta and worked closely with state and local public health departments. At the end of the war, the MCWA became a permanent agency of the PHS as the Communicable Disease Center and, subsequently, the Centers for Disease Control. The moving force behind the MCWA and its conversion to the CDC was Dr. Joseph Mountin (above).

PHS improved and regularized nursing education, and scholastic and construction grants to nursing schools enabled many of them to emerge from the shadows of the hospitals that previously had been their sole sponsors. The profession of nursing established itself as a strong and permanent presence within the PHS with Lucile Petry Leone becoming the first nurse and the first woman to achieve the rank of Assistant Surgeon General (the equivalent of Rear Admiral) in 1949. Her appointment made her the first woman in the uniformed services of the United States to achieve flag rank.[15]

The war years had an enormous impact on the PHS. Not only did the war require expansion of its programs and personnel, but the PHS Act of 1944 effected organizational changes that the Service had long sought. The law broadened the Commissioned Corps, authorizing the commissioning of nurses, scientists, dieticians, physical therapists, and sanitarians. The sanitarian category was later divided into health service officers and sanitarians. Veterinarians subsequently became eligible for commissions as well. During the war, John Eason was commissioned as the Service's first black officer. A Howard-trained bacteriologist, Eason's initial assignment to Baltimore had to be cancelled because the health department there refused to accept a black officer in uniform. He served with the state health department in Kentucky instead.[16]

The 1944 Act also specified a new organization for the PHS. The Office of the Surgeon General and three "bureaus"—State Services, Medical Services, and the NIH—were required by the law and served as the administrative structure for the activities of the PHS for the ensuing twenty years. From 1940 to 1945, the PHS as a whole doubled in size to 16,000 while the Commissioned Corps quadrupled its numbers from 625 officers to 2,600. Moreover, PHS wartime growth proved to be permanent, with little attrition in the total size of the Service occurring as the nation demobilized. The Commissioned Corps that emerged from the war was a different organization from the one that had previously existed. Two-thirds of its officers were in the reserve corps, one-half were non-physicians and almost one-quarter were women. While there would be fluctuations in these balances in future years, the small, predominantly male, career, doctor brigade of the past was gone forever. Federal public health had a new identity and a new standing in postwar America.

The involvement of the PHS with global public health during the war, as well as the development of the United Nations in the postwar period, led to a variety of international activities. The Surgeon General formed an Office of International Health Relations which worked extensively with Liberia, Greece, and Iran over the following years to develop public health systems in those nations. Working un-

Building rat traps (above), trapping the rats, and dusting the rat runs with DDT were the essence of typhus control. This work was assigned to the MCWA late in the war as was responsibility for research on flea- and fly-borne diseases and tropical parasites, paving the way for the transformation of the MCWA into the CDC in 1946.

der the auspices of the Economic and Social Council of the United Nations, the International Health Conference that convened in New York in June, 1946 elected Parran its president and proceeded to draft a constitution for a World Health Organization. It took two years of diplomacy by Parran to reach agreement among participating countries and with existing international health groups. The Pan American Sanitary Bureau, headed by former Surgeon General Hugh Cumming, was particularly reluctant to forego its independence in favor of the global organization. At length accord was reached and on April 7, 1948, the World Health Organization was born.

The PHS's largest institutional legacy from the Second World War started quietly in Atlanta. Malaria in the southern United States continued to pose a problem for the war effort due to the concentration of military facilities in the area. In 1942, the PHS began a campaign, using larvicide and swamp drainage, aimed at controlling malaria throughout the South and in the Caribbean. The effort was called the Malaria Control in War Areas (MCWA) program. By 1943, the Atlanta-based initiative employed 4,300 people including 300 commissioned officers, many of whom were engineers and sanitarians. The MCWA took on typhus control and staged training courses in tropical diseases in anticipation of servicemen returning with illnesses unfamiliar to American clinicians. By its nature, much of this work involved collaborative activities with state and local health departments for whom the MCWA began to serve as a regular consultant.

It was Joseph Mountin's vision that the MCWA should have a life beyond the war. As director of the Bureau of State Services, he supervised the Atlanta program and saw its potential as a permanent asset to national public health, monitoring infectious disease problems, providing education and support to local health units, and engaging in field research that was less suited to the laboratory-oriented NIH. This latter point was a delicate one inasmuch as the NIH was the PHS's designated research institution; yet its increased focus on basic science and chronic disease and its growing reliance on laboratory-based technology had left a void in the PHS. After much debate on names, Mountin and MCWA director, Mark Hollis, proposed that the MCWA be designated as the Communicable Disease Center (CDC), persuaded Parran and NIH Director Rolla E. Dyer of the wisdom of this idea, and obtained congressional consent. On July 1, 1946, the MCWA became the CDC with Hollis as its first director.[17]

Two pieces of legislation that had been debated during the war years but had to await the peace for enactment were passed in 1946. The first was the Hill-Burton Act. Although the postwar Congress could not reach consensus on the financing of medical care, it did agree on a large federal incentive program for the building of hospitals—the Hospital Survey and Construction Act of 1946. Funded by

The increase in international air travel increased concern about the rapid spread of epidemic disease and, particularly, the possibility of importing yellow fever from South America. The PHS inspected planes (opposite below right), sprayed the cabins of aircraft (opposite above) with insecticide, and examined passengers on arrival (opposite below left).

PHS in response to state plans, Hill-Burton guaranteed PHS involvement in hospital construction and policy for many years in the future. Between 1947 and 1971, the $3.7 billion disbursed under the program paid for 10 percent of all hospital construction in the United States and was matched by $9.1 billion in state funds.[18]

The second key bill of 1946 was largely the work of Robert Felix, a PHS psychiatrist trained by Treadway and Kolb, who had been the chief of the Mental Hygiene Division since 1944. Felix wanted to move toward a national mental health program, founded on research and built on a base of community care. To achieve this, he reasoned, an expanded program of training for mental health professionals would have to be developed. The National Mental Health Act of 1946, in fact, authorized research, training, and aid to states for services but it passed without an appropriation. Not wanting to lose the momentum behind the Act, Felix raised $15,000 from a private foundation to hold the first meeting of the Mental Health Advisory Board called for in the legislation. In 1948, Congress appropriated money for the law and in 1949 the National Institute of Mental Health (NIMH) opened for business at the NIH with Felix as its director.

Teeth that were black and mottled but had no caries (opposite above left) were the result of elevated natural fluoride in drinking water. This phenomenon led NIH dental scientist Dr. H. Trendley Dean (above foreground) to the use of water fluoridation to prevent caries, a proposition first tested on a large scale in Grand Rapids, Michigan (telegram opposite above) in 1944. School children in Grand Rapids provide saliva samples (opposite below) as part of that city's water fluoridation project.

The years of the 1930s and the 1940s were ones of calamity and necessity for the United States. The Depression and the Second World War were calamities that affected virtually the entire society and made solutions politically and socially feasible that might not have been possible under less adverse conditions. In the domain of the PHS, the Social Security Act with all of its ramifications, the Cadet Nurse Corps and its legacy for American nursing, the MCWA and its evolution into the CDC, and even the World Health Organization, were the products of necessity. The PHS under Parran's leadership successfully converted adversity into opportunity and significantly increased the role of federal public health in the life of the nation.

By 1948, however, the Depression and the war were history. The vision of a national health system shared by Parran and other public health progressives had not been realized, and though the PHS had grown significantly in size, it was still not a national health department. The Marine Hospitals remained the largest employer within the PHS but their very existence would soon be questioned by a commission chaired by former President Hoover—the first of many such challenges to the hospitals. Roosevelt, Parran's friend and mentor, had died in 1945 and relations between Parran and his immediate boss, the FSA administrator Oscar Ewing, were not good. In April of 1948, Truman declined to reappoint Parran to a fourth term as Surgeon General, bringing to a close both an epoch in the history of the Public Health Service and an extraordinary PHS career.

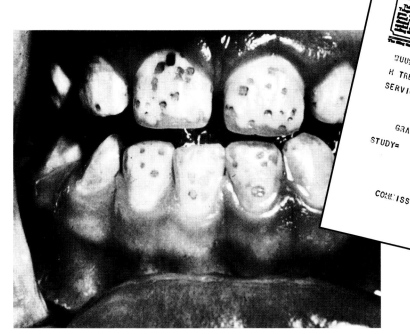

The Coming of HEW

On the surface, the years between 1949 and 1960 were quiescent ones for the PHS. The social activism of the New Deal and the governmental pragmatism of the war were in the past and the titanic struggles over the medical care of the elderly and the poor were yet to come. Yet the expansion of the Public Health Service in the 1950s was real, with annual appropriations quadrupling to $840 million by the end of the Eisenhower administration. Substantial budget increases and the addition of new institutes to the NIH led this trend, but the programs of the PHS as a whole continued to grow both by expansion and acquisition. Simultaneously, a subtle transition was taking place in which politics was exerting an ever stronger influence on the domain of federal public health and the corps of career officers who managed it. While little would change initially, the Eisenhower administration's replacement of the FSA with the Department of Health, Education, and Welfare would be a bureaucratic transformation that contained the elements of a radical redefinition of the Public Health Service.

President Truman's choice to replace Surgeon General Parran was Dr. Leonard Scheele, the director of the National Cancer Institute. If Parran's strong suit was public health practice, Scheele's was medical research, and his appointment reflected the growing prominence of research in the domain of public health. Scheele began his PHS career as an intern at the Chicago Marine Hospital in 1933, worked in foreign quarantine, and as the health officer of Queen Anne's County, Maryland. Joseph Mountin selected Scheele in 1936 and sent him to Memorial Hospital in New York to be trained in cancer research, after which he was assigned to the NCI. Following Second World War service in Europe, Scheele returned to the NCI, first as its assistant director and then, in 1947, as its director.

Scheele brought to the job vocational and political perspectives well suited to the times. Aided by the philanthropist team of Albert and Mary Lasker as well as Senator Lister Hill and Representative John Fogarty, the rate of growth of the NIH began a spectacular climb in the late 1940s. Within Scheele's first year in office, two new institutes were signed into law (the National Heart Institute and the National Institute of Dental Research), the NIH name was made plural (the National Institutes of Health), and $40 million was appropriated to build a research hospital on the campus to be called the Clinical Center. Four more institutes would be added and the NIH budget

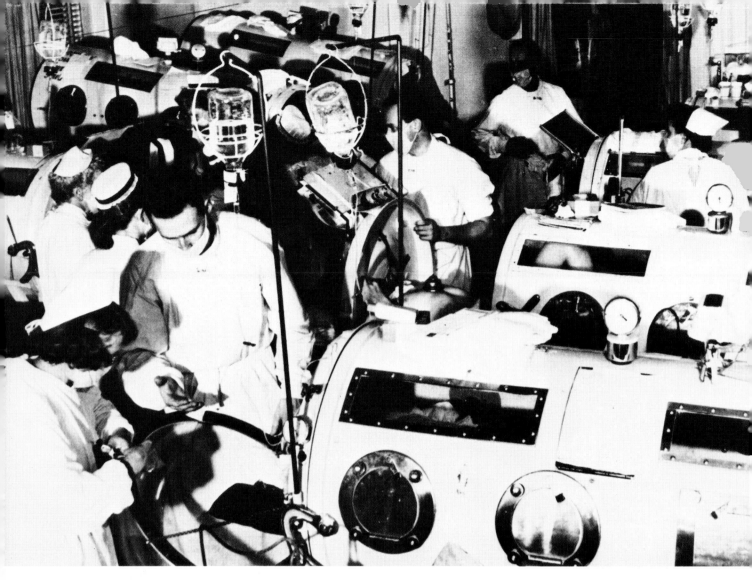

would grow from $37 million to almost $100 million during the seven years of Scheele's tenure.[1]

His politics were strikingly different from those of his predecessor who was clearly Democratic in affiliation and activist in style. "My politics didn't get me the job because they couldn't tell my politics," Scheele commented in retrospect. "As a matter of fact, I, like most people in the Public Health Service in those days, only voted in national elections."[2] Scheele chose not to get involved in the last chapter of the Murray-Wagner-Dingell debate, which occurred around the National Health Assembly held in May of 1948, at which time the Truman administration struggled to gain an endorsement for national health insurance and the AMA fought hard against "state medicine." Federal Security Agency Administrator Oscar Ewing asked Scheele to go on television with him to debate with the AMA. Scheele refused stating, "The minute I do that I'm finished as a professional officer for you, and you want the Surgeon General's job to stay a professional officer's job, so I think you've got to find somebody else."[3] Ewing accepted Scheele's refusal.

The coming of the Korean War and the rise of Senator Joseph McCarthy contributed to the increasingly conservative political climate of the country. National health insurance was dead, the AMA redoubled its campaign against "socialized medicine" and the repercussions of McCarthyism reached the PHS with loyalty investigations, dismissals, and instances of political interference with extramural grants.[4] Through the battles over health insurance, organized medicine had served notice on the PHS that medical care was the domain of private medicine. This political environment, combined with the traditionalist roots of many Service officers and the clearly articulated philosophy of the Surgeon General that speaking out on matters of health insurance would be "nonprofessional," limited the role of the PHS in regard to medical care policy. Medical research, on the other hand, was a promising and politically neutral domain of governmental activity and it grew accordingly.

Before the introduction of the Salk and Sabin vaccines against polio in the 1950s, the iron lung (opposite above) and children in braces (opposite below) were common phenomena. Dr. Leonard Scheele served as Surgeon General from 1948 to 1956 and participated in the decisions concerning the first large-scale polio vaccination campaign in 1955. He is pictured above (left) with the PHS Chief Nurse Officer Lucile Petry Leone (right) and a visiting French nurse (center).

O n assuming office in 1953, President Eisenhower moved quickly to elevate the FSA to cabinet status as the Department of Health, Education, and Welfare, a move previously opposed by Republicans but one that the new president thought to be timely. In order to avoid controversy since he was reorganizing by executive authority rather than by legislative mandate, no substantial changes were made in the structure of the FSA. The Surgeon General would report to the new secretary who was Oveta Culp Hobby, a Democrat, an old friend of President Eisenhower, and the only woman in the cabinet. Since no laws were rewritten, all of the authorities of the Surgeon General remained intact and

For many years, the PHS participated informally in the provision of health care to American Indians and Alaska Natives. Dr. Ralph Carr (above) examines children while ashore from a Coast Guard cutter in Ketchikan, Alaska in 1941. In 1954 Congress formally transferred care of Native Americans from the Bureau of Indian Affairs to the Indian Health Service.

were not transferred to the secretary—a point that would cause problems for later secretaries.

In deference to the AMA's stated desire to have a designated physician high in the ranks of the new department, Hobby created a staff position called "Special Assistant to the Secretary for Health and Medical Affairs." In the early years of HEW, this was a relatively unimportant post with the Surgeon General, a career officer and the legally specified executor of the public health duties of the department, remaining as the line manager with authority over the PHS. The Special Assistant position, however, held the germ of a new concept—the political management of federal public health. The individuals filling the Special Assistant role who were, of course, political appointees, became increasingly important players within the department and, by the early 1960s, the relative merits of politically appointed versus career leadership of the PHS became a topical and, ultimately, critical issue.[5]

The relationship between scientific practice and politics was put to an early and tough test in the new department in the events that surrounded the introduction of Salk polio vaccine in the spring of 1955. Polio was a widely and properly feared disease in the early 1950s with thousands of paralytic cases occurring annually. The news of a vaccine developed by Jonas Salk, backed by the National Foundation for Infantile Paralysis (popularly known as the March of Dimes), which was the subject of a massive clinical trial in early 1954, was closely followed by the press and the public. Despite the concern of some scientists that the agent was being rushed into use because of public pressure and without adequate testing, the NIH and Scheele endorsed the vaccine based on their analyses of the clinical trial data and, on April 12, 1955, Secretary Hobby issued licenses to six pharmaceutical companies to begin distribution.

Two weeks later, cases of polio in newly vaccinated children began to be reported from various parts of the country, turning the excitement of the nation to alarm, and putting the department and the PHS at the center of a fierce scientific and political controversy as to the cause of the problem and whether to halt the vaccination campaign or not. On May 7th, Scheele issued a statement urging the postponement of all polio vaccination activities while the vaccine was reexamined. Within a short period, vaccine produced by Cutter Laboratories was identified as the principal source of the iatrogenic polio. Seventy-one cases of paralytic polio had occurred and eleven children died.[6]

The political fallout of "the Cutter incident" was significant, with the press and the Congress directing criticism at HEW. According to Scheele, the secretary took the brunt of the rebukes. "During the vaccine period she (Hobby) was very heavily attacked. I as an M.D. and a public health person by and large was not attacked. . . .

Mrs. Hobby had signed the approval of the vaccine, so she was equally involved in that process. She couldn't say, 'Well, I didn't do it.' So she was attacked politically and otherwise."[7] Although some dispute the reasons for their departures, Hobby and her Special Assistant for Health and Medical Affairs both resigned within the next two months, apparently as a result of the Cutter incident. If the careers of political appointees were going to ride on the work of a career service, the PHS, would there not soon be the demand that its leadership be political as well?

Intensive efforts to bring down the high rates of tuberculosis (above) and infant mortality were notable early successes of the IHS. The mobility of the Commissioned Corps contributed to the ability of the Service to provide care where it was most needed. A PHS physician (opposite) makes a house call on the floor of the Grand Canyon.

In 1955, the PHS became doctor to the Indians of America. The federal government, in fact, had been involved with the health of Indians since 1802 when Army doctors inoculated tribes around military camps in the West during smallpox epidemics. With the transfer of the Bureau of Indian Affairs (BIA) from the War Department to the Department of the Interior in 1849, there were sporadic efforts to hire physicians and provide preventive care to Indian populations. By 1926, a more organized BIA began to call on the PHS to provide physicians as consultants and health program administrators and, following a 1936 survey by Service officers Joseph Mountin and J.G. Townsend, an unsuccessful attempt was made to transfer Indian health care to the PHS.

By all standards, the patchwork of services provided to the Indians by the BIA was poor. In 1949, for example, the BIA employed ninety-six full time physicians to staff eighty-one hospitals for 500,000 Indians. Infant mortality among Indians was more than double that of the general population and life expectancy was a decade less than the rest of the nation. Tuberculosis was rampant with 10 percent of Alaska Natives examined for military service during the Second World War having active tuberculosis. This latter fact stimulated the National Tuberculosis Association to begin a campaign in 1949 that included the AMA, the American Public Health Association, and the Association of State and Territorial Health Officials to put the PHS in charge of Indian health care. The belief was that since health was but one concern among many at the BIA, the agency would never be able to retain competent physicians or run a quality health care system. These arguments were backed by the senior PHS officers assigned to the BIA from 1948 to 1955, Drs. Fred Foard and Ray Shaw, the latter of whom complained bitterly about the tuberculosis funds for the Gallup, New Mexico area being converted into a warehouse and a community center. "If real progress was to be made," he claimed, "the (Indian) health program had to be controlled by health people who would make the decisions, make the allocations, do the recruitment, promotion of support services of all kinds and, quite frankly, the sooner we got out of the BIA, the better."[8]

Ford's Theater, site of the Library of the Army Surgeon General from 1866 to 1887.

Medical Knowledge —Past and Future The National Library of Medicine

The largest medical library in the world, the National Library of Medicine, is part of the Public Health Service. Although books were collected earlier, the formal library dates from 1836 when the office of the Surgeon General of the Army began to purchase medical volumes. By the end of the Civil War, the collection had grown to 2,000 books and was put in the care of John Shaw Billings—an extraordinary young Army physician whose early work included a critical evaluation of the marine hospitals that led to the formation of the Marine Hospital Service in 1870. Billings decided that the library should be as complete as possible and, to that end, he began to collect both new and old biomedical publications.

After President Abraham Lincoln was assassinated in Ford's Theater in

1865, the theater was closed as a place of entertainment and became the home of the Army Medical Museum and the Library of the Surgeon General's Office. By 1875, Billings' labors had resulted in the acquisition of 75 percent of the medical journals of the time and he embarked on a new enterprise—the cataloguing of the medical literature. His *Index-Catalogue* provided information about the library's holdings while his monthly *Index Medicus*—which is still published today—was a timely guide to recent publications. These bibliographic tools made the medical literature far more accessible than it had ever been. Billings next obtained funds for better quarters from Congress, opening a new building on the Mall in 1887 that was known affectionately as "The Old Red Brick."

Billings retired in 1895 and the library endured a period of relative stagnation until after the Second World War when the demand for medical information increased. In 1949, Dr. Frank Rogers became director and the library began a period of major change. The National Library of Medicine

(NLM) Act of 1956 transferred the institution from the Armed Forces to the PHS, established a Board of Regents for it, and authorized the construction of a new facility. Rogers oversaw the opening of the new library building in 1962 on the campus of the NIH in Bethesda, Maryland, and began to explore the use of computerized systems to sort and arrange the library's citations. In 1964, during the directorship of Dr. Martin Cummings, the NLM implemented the Medical Literature Analysis and Retrieval System (MEDLARS), a computerized system to organize and disseminate references to the medical literature. The addition in 1968 of a research and development capability— the Lister Hill National Center for Biomedical Communications—helped transform the NLM into a center for information science. In the following years, MEDLARS spawned a variety of more specialized, electronic data bases (including one with the clever name of "Grateful Med") which now permit nearly twelve million references to be searched by personal computer from anywhere in the United States.

Serving as the core of a system of 7 regional, 125 medical school, and 4,000 health science libraries across the nation, today's NLM is a participant in the global project to map the human genome and a leader in the physical preservation of biomedical literature. "Medical informatics"—the science of biomedical information management and transfer—is at the heart of the NLM's current programs. Dr. Donald Lindberg, library director since 1984, has emphasized the exploration of new forms of electronic knowledge management through the use of artificial intelligence, videodiscs, a unified medical language system, and advanced biotechnology data bases. John Shaw Billings would be pleased with what has become of his library.

The main reading room in the "Old Red Brick," home of the Library from 1887 to 1962.

The National Library of Medicine in Bethesda, Maryland opened in 1962.

NLM's computer center in the 1960s.

Dr. Leroy Burney (opposite) devoted considerable attention to environmental matters during his tenure as Surgeon General from 1956 to 1961. As part of the environmental activities of the PHS, radiation and its biological effects were studied (right) and in 1957 a Division of Radiation Health was established. With the mushroom cloud behind them (above), staff from the PHS and the military measure radiation levels during atmospheric weapons testing in the central Pacific in 1962. Pictured (left to right) are Lt. Joseph Hans, PHS; Maj. Knipp, USA; Capt. Henry Rechen, PHS; and Yeoman King, USN.

That, simply, was the intent of the Transfer Act of 1954 which proposed moving all Indian health programs and responsibilities from the BIA to a new Division of Indian Health in the PHS. The legislation was opposed by the Bureau of the Budget who thought it would cost more, some Oklahoma tribes who thought they would get less, and HEW, which argued that the move would not solve and might even aggravate Indian health problems. Nonetheless, the forces behind the move prevailed and on July 1, 1955, the Indian Health Service (IHS) came into being. On that date, the PHS inherited from the BIA 2,500 staff, 48 hospitals, 13 school infirmaries and the responsibility for 472,000 Indians and 35,000 Alaska Natives. Shaw became the IHS director, stating that his first two program goals were "to do things *with* people rather than *to* them . . . (and) to bring tuberculosis under control."[9]

Congress supported the Indian Health Service from the outset. The 1955 appropriation of $36 million was double that of the year before and support continued to grow annually thereafter. The 1957 Indian Health Facilities Act and the 1959 Indian Sanitation Facilities Construction Act initiated large-scale campaigns of hospital building and the construction of water supply and waste disposal systems in Indian communities and homes. The IHS ran orientation programs for its employees that emphasized cross-cultural cooperation and taught the joint practice of public health and medical care. To set the tone of the IHS, Shaw was fond of quoting the Chinese proverb, "Tell me, I'll forget; show me, I may remember; but involve me and I'll understand." By 1960, the infant mortality rate had declined by almost 25 percent and the death rate from tuberculosis by almost 50 percent. The premise of those who had argued for the Transfer Act—that the PHS could improve the health of Indians—was borne out.

The CDC's Epidemic Intelligence Service (EIS), established in 1951, signalled much about the future of the Atlanta-based agency as a national and global resource for applied public health. Alexander Langmuir, a physician trained in Wade Hampton Frost's department at Johns Hopkins, joined the CDC staff in 1949 for the purpose of developing an epidemiology division. His interest in epidemiological detective work ("shoe leather epidemiology," as it came to be called) gained support due, in part, to the growing concern with biological warfare at the time of the Korean War. It was Joseph Mountin, himself, who suggested to Langmuir the name "Epidemic Intelligence Service" during discussions about the recruitment and training of a team of epidemiologists prepared to deal with infectious disease emergencies.

Langmuir had a much broader concept in mind than a biological warfare surveillance unit. In July of 1951, twenty-three recruits ar-

A noxious smog killed 120 people and made 6,000 ill in the steel town of Donora, Pennsylvania, in 1948. The PHS fielded a 25-man team to investigate. PHS engineer George Clayton (above) prepares an air quality measuring device on a hill overlooking a smog-shrouded valley at Donora. Clayton and chemist Harold Paulus (left) set up equipment to test air quality near the zinc plant suspected of causing the smog.

rived in Atlanta to begin a six-week epidemiological crash course run by Langmuir and taught by borrowed Hopkins faculty members. According to William Stewart, a member of the first EIS class and a future Surgeon General, Langmuir's "basic idea (was) that you develop a corps for the United States who had enough knowledge about epidemiology and statistics to go out and investigate epidemics. He also wanted to have them stationed somewhere else, such as in the states. I ended up at the Thomasville, Georgia, field station investigating diarrheal diseases."[10] Although the class size has more than tripled in the years since, the basic formula of short, intensive training at the CDC, followed by assignments to operating public health units of the PHS, to state or municipal government, has remained unaltered to the present. Epidemic Intelligence Service assignees are on permanent call and are dispatched quickly by the CDC to disease outbreak sites. "State health officers were astounded to find bright, young, responsive epidemiologists in their offices the next morning, or even sometimes the same day that they called," reported Langmuir of his program. "Each epidemic aid call was an adventure and a training experience, even the false alarms."[11] Over the years, the alumni of the EIS have staffed not only the CDC but also health departments and academic infectious disease departments throughout the country.

The growth of the EIS was but one aspect of CDC's overall expansion during the 1950s. Amidst protests from longtime workers, the PHS' Venereal Disease Division moved to Atlanta from Washington in 1957 followed by the Tuberculosis Division in 1960. The former brought with it a new and important category of PHS worker, the public health advisor. Hired first in 1948 on an experimental basis that proved extremely successful, these workers were college graduates without professional credentials, trained to do venereal disease interviews and contact tracing. As a group, they became versatile CDC workers, staffing not only the venereal disease program but also the immunization program and, eventually, the administration of the CDC itself. In the summer of 1960, the CDC moved into newly built and much-expanded quarters in Atlanta on Clifton Road adjacent to Emory University. Langmuir's continued consolidation of an epidemiological power center was aided by the CDC's acquisition in 1961 of the historic but lifeless Morbidity and Mortality Weekly Report, to be revitalized by the Epidemiology Branch as a popular and much-cited national publication.

In August of 1956, Scheele retired and was replaced by Leroy Burney, a twenty-four-year veteran of the Service who began his career as a Marine Hospital intern—the last of the Surgeons General to do so. Burney had done rural venereal disease work in the South in the 1930s, worked abroad for the War Shipping Ad-

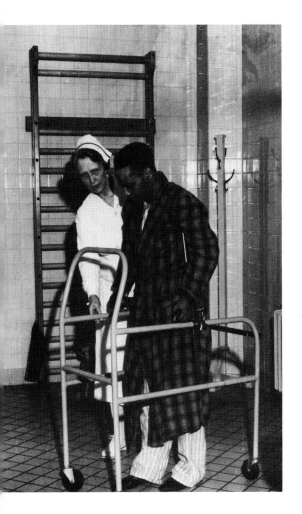

The PHS hospitals and clinics continued to provide care for members of the merchant marine, the Coast Guard, and the military. A Coast Guard helicopter delivers victims of a collision in New York harbor to the Staten Island Hospital (opposite above). Physical therapy was an important component of the hospitals' program. A patient receives a "Scotch douche" (opposite below right), a hydrotherapy treatment for back spasms, while another (above) learns to walk again. A pharmacist (opposite below left) prepares an intravenous solution at the NIH Clinical Center, the research hospital opened on the Bethesda campus in 1953.

ministration, and served on detail from the PHS as the state health commissioner of Indiana from 1945 to 1954. In addition to continued growth occurring in major areas of the PHS, his tenure was marked by challenges developing in two important, traditional areas of PHS activity—environmental health and the Marine Hospitals.

Although the term "environmental health" had been used before the 1950s, it was only during this decade that the full breadth of the damage that man could do to the environment was understood by scientists, politicians and, ultimately, the public. Studies of water quality, dating from the PHS Act of 1912, and the subsequent work of the Stream Pollution Investigations Station at Cincinnati focused on fecal contamination of water supplies. Surgeon General Parran, fond of remarking that "flushing a toilet does not end the problem of the proper disposal of wastes," lobbied hard for the first comprehensive Water Pollution Control Act that passed in 1948. As a result of the 1948 law, the PHS's chief engineer and former CDC director, Mark Hollis, set to work with Joseph Mountin planning a new environmental health installation to replace the aging Cincinnati laboratory. This facility opened in 1954 as the Robert A. Taft Sanitary Engineering Center.

By the middle of the decade, growing evidence of chemicals in the water supply, rapidly deteriorating urban air quality, and the accumulating evidence of radiation in the atmosphere from nuclear weapons testing combined to focus attention on the environment in an expanded and urgent fashion. Surgeon General Burney made a number of moves in response to these developments. He appointed a National Advisory Committee on Radiation and followed its recommendations by creating a Division of Radiological Health to unify radiation-related PHS activities. He recruited the interest of the powerful Congressman, John Fogarty, who, as late as 1957, told Burney that he did not know what the term "environmental health" meant. Burney recalls taking him to dinner at Fort McNair to explain and coming away with the invitation "to put (some language) in the appropriations hearings."[12] That discussion led to Fogarty's permanent interest in the environment and to the appointment—thanks to "the language"— of a committee of experts to advise the PHS and the Congress on environmental matters.

The PHS, nonetheless, had difficulty in satisfying the expectations of the developing environmental lobby. As early as 1954, cuts in the water pollution control budget elicited criticism of the PHS from groups concerned with the environment. By the 1960 presidential campaign, serious proposals were pending in Congress that would remove water pollution control from the PHS on the grounds that it involved conservation and wildlife concerns as well as sewage treatment.[13] Burney, himself, noted that there was an important difference between the PHS' familiar ground of fighting infectious

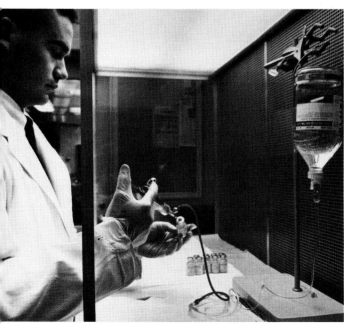

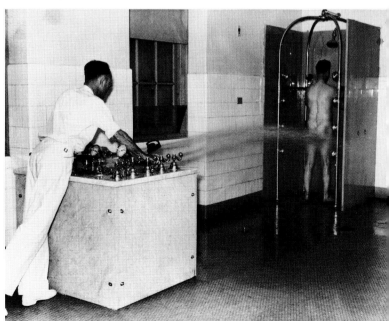

disease and the newer role of defending the environment. "When we are dealing with the possible harmful effects of the byproducts of industry and the wastes of nuclear technology, our goal is not conquest but containment."[14] Because "containment" was a less precise concept than "conquest" and, therefore, subject to greater contention, the domain of environmental protection was destined to become steadily more political even as the tools of environmental science improved.

Toward the end of the decade, medical care reemerged as an important national policy issue. Older Americans, in particular, who had not benefitted from the vast movement toward job-related, voluntary health insurance, were vociferous about their need for government assistance. The Social Security Administration, however, and not the PHS was the principal HEW agency involved in these debates. The PHS was struggling with new challenges to its own hospital system. Scrutiny of the Marine Hospitals began with a 1949 report to Congress by a commission chaired by Herbert Hoover that recommended folding all government health care into a "United Medical Administration." Although this proposal never went far, it did inaugurate what proved to be a thirty-year crusade by the Bureau of the Budget to close the PHS hospitals. Why should the American sailors receive federal medical care, their argument ran, when other workers were negotiating health insurance as an employment benefit? Implicit in this challenge, of course, was the related query: why a Commissioned Corps at all? Between 1948 and 1956, five of the extant twenty-one hospitals were closed, leading Burney to report to HEW Secretary Marion Folsom that "We (are) creating a ring of second class hospitals. . . . We should either get in and do a good job or get out."[15] Folsom supported Burney and the hospitals stayed open but they would remain embattled institutions.

In recognition of the changes that were taking place, Burney appointed a "Study Group on Mission and Organization of the Public Health Service" which reported its findings in June of 1960. They wrote that:

> The next great nationwide health efforts may be expected in two broad areas: the physical environment and comprehensive health care. During the present decade, 1960-1970, major national efforts, comparable with the great expansions of medical research and hospitals in the 1950s, will be required in each of these areas.[16]

They were absolutely right in their prediction but the report did not foresee how large and how political those new "nationwide health efforts" would be. Not only would the legislative activism of the next decade generate new environmental and community health programs, it would place many of them in agencies of government other than the PHS. Health would move to the center of the national stage in the 1960s and, paradoxically, threaten the very existence of the Public Health Service.

During the postwar period, the PHS was active in international health work. A malaria control worker (opposite above right), assigned to the World Health Organization, draws blood in Ethiopia in 1954, while PHS sanitarians identify mosquitos in an insect control course in 1950 (opposite below right). George Moore, a PHS medical officer (opposite far left), participates in a malaria survey in Nepal in 1953. On the trail, he used the rifle for protection against "leopards, bears and guerrillas" and to augment the party's food supply. Dr. Hildrus A. Poindexter (above) came to the PHS after the Second World War already well-known as a tropical disease expert. He headed the PHS Mission to Liberia and served as well in Surinam, Iraq, Libya, Jamaica, and Sierra Leone.

Public Health
At The
New Frontier

Campaigning for the presidency in 1960, John Kennedy pledged "to get the country moving again," to rekindle the intellectual and legislative dynamism of former years and to break away from what many felt to be the economic and social stagnation of the 1950s. Touting space exploration, economic growth, and social progress, he called his program the "New Frontier." Kennedy narrowly won the election but his youthful vigor, evident idealism, and imaginative programs quickly won him broad popularity. He backed technology, committing the United States to put a man on the moon by the end of the decade, as well as social reform, arguing that with 20 percent of Americans living below the poverty line, the "culture of poverty" would be a target of his administration. He pledged, in particular, to enact a program of medical care for the aged under the Social Security system. On the domestic side, though, he was faced with the same congressional coalition of Southern Democrats and Republicans that had dominated policy during the previous years, and whose politics were far more conservative than his own. Kennedy labored hard during his presidency to turn health and social reform ideas into law. Ultimately, these programs would be his legacy much more than his achievement, having a far greater effect on the PHS after his death than during his presidency.

For the first time in history, the completion of the four-year term of the Surgeon General coincided with the arrival of a new political administration. Kennedy's HEW secretary, Abraham Ribicoff, did not reappoint Leroy Burney but reached down into the ranks of the PHS to choose a relatively junior officer, Dr. Luther Terry, to replace him. Terry came from Alabama where his father had been a physician and close friend of a noted local surgeon, Dr. Luther Leonidas Hill, after whom the younger Terry was named. Dr. Hill's son went into politics, and by 1960 was the principal health power in Congress, Senator Lister Hill. The younger Terry studied medicine, joined the PHS in 1942 serving at the Baltimore Marine Hospital and, in 1948, started a cardiovascular research service there. With the opening of the NIH Clinical Center in 1953, Terry's unit was moved to the Heart Institute of which he became deputy director in 1958—the position he held when he was appointed Surgeon General.

Terry took charge of a PHS comprised of 24,000 civil service employees and 4,000 commissioned officers arrayed in three agencies— the Bureau of State Services, the Bureau of Medical Services, and the

*The PHS launched the national
campaign against smoking (opposite) in
1964.*

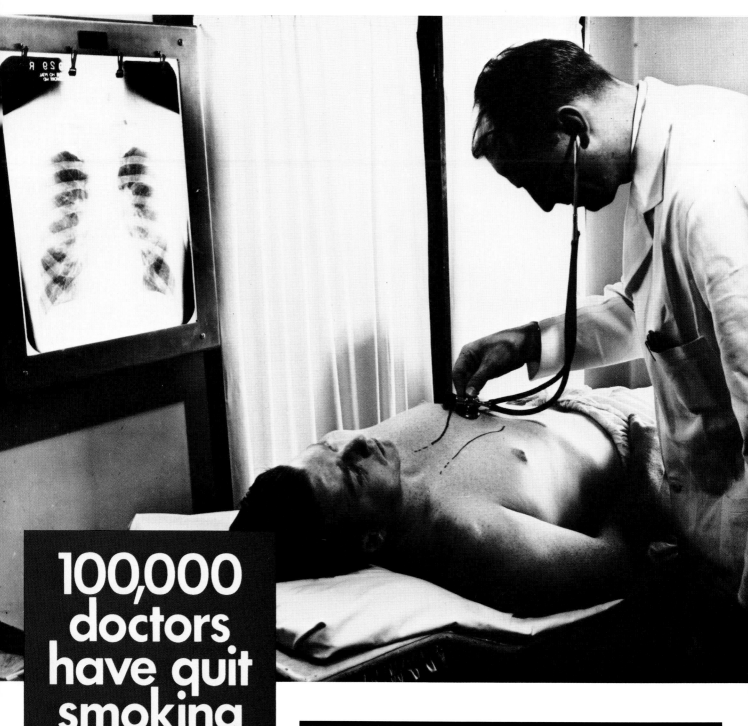

100,000 doctors have quit smoking cigarettes.

(Maybe they know something you don't.)

Although smoking had been a concern of the PHS for many years and Surgeon General Leroy Burney had published a major summary of its deleterious effects in 1959, the 1964 report Smoking and Health (opposite) captured the permanent attention of physicians (poster left) and the nation. The force behind the report was Dr. Luther Terry (above examining patient) who was deputy director of the National Heart Institute before serving as Surgeon General from 1961 to 1965.

rapidly expanding NIH. Indeed, Terry was the first of three successive Surgeons General who acceded to the post from positions at the NIH, suggesting the enormous force that the NIH had become within the PHS. Since 1955, NIH Director Dr. James Shannon had skillfully orchestrated the aspirations for growth within the NIH, the friendly external pressures applied by the Laskers and their allies, and the enormous funding power of Hill and Fogarty in the Congress. The result was NIH growth from $100 million in 1955 to $1 billion a decade later, a figure representing almost one-half of the PHS budget. "Then, the Congress and NIH were writing the budget," recollects Dr. William Stewart.

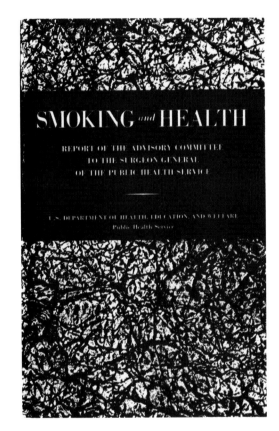

> This extended into Kennedy's term. Kennedy, I think, stopped it by one of the years giving them everything they asked for and they had more than they could handle, and he got control of the budget. There was a three or four year period in there when the Department had no say in the NIH budget.[1]

Although Terry's roots were at the NIH, his most celebrated achievement was in the translation of research findings into public health policy. As early as 1956, the PHS in conjunction with the American Cancer Society (ACS) and the American Heart Association (AHA), had established a study group on smoking and health. In 1959, Surgeon General Burney published an article in the Journal of the American Medical Association entitled "Smoking and Lung Cancer: A Statement of the Public Health Service" which concluded that "The weight of evidence at present implicates smoking as the principal etiological factor in the increased incidence of lung cancer."[2]

Pressured by the tobacco industry on one side and the ACS and the AHA on the other, the PHS took the issue up again in 1962, when Terry appointed a ten-person Advisory Committee on Smoking and Health. Based at the National Library of Medicine, the committee met regularly between November of 1962 and December of 1963, during which time they reviewed all available animal, clinical, and epidemiological studies on the effects of smoking. Unlike Burney's earlier report, Terry's announcement of the committee's findings in January of 1964 played to a standing-room-only press conference held on a Saturday to minimize the impact on tobacco stocks. "Cigarette smoking is causally related to lung cancer in men," Terry stated bluntly. "The magnitude of the effect of cigarette smoking far outweighs all other factors. The data for women, though less extensive, point in the same direction."[3]

The Federal Trade Commission as well as the Congress responded quickly to the report, the former calling for warning labels on cigarette packages and the latter passing legislation to require it. Warning requirements were subsequently added to cigarette advertising and the warnings themselves strengthened. Terry's leadership of the antismoking forces propelled him onto the national stage and added a new and, and as it turned out, permanent role to the office of the Surgeon General. "After (the report), everything was speeches on that, every press release, every press conference," recalls Terry's associate and successor, William Stewart, whose tenure began before the initial legislation was passed. "Everywhere I went, every press conference was on smoking....When I testified in Congress there were major attacks on me. The man from North Carolina came into the hearing with a tobacco plant in a pot and he said, 'This man is trying to kill this beautiful plant'....I wasn't welcomed in North Carolina at all."[4] From Terry's report on, the role of the Surgeon General has been inextricably tied to the campaign against smoking.[5]

The years of the Kennedy administration were ones of cautious legislative stirrings in a number of health areas. A decade earlier, a report to President Truman entitled *Building America's Health* had pointed to the need to expand the nation's medical training capabilities and was echoed by a 1958 study done for the PHS that called for the expansion of existing schools and the construction of new ones. Political pressure mounted as hundreds of American communities and scores of legislators registered complaints at the lack of family doctors. The Health Professions Educational Assistance Act of 1963 provided funds for new schools and incentives for increased enrollment in extant ones and began a quiet revolution in health manpower sponsored by the PHS. It was followed by the Nurse Training Act of 1964 and the Allied Health Professions Training Act of 1966. Between the mid-1960s and 1980, the United States doubled the number of physicians and substantially increased the numbers of nurses and dentists graduated annually, alleviating shortages in more affluent communities and making possible programs to address medical underservice in poor areas.[6]

The assassination of John Kennedy in November of 1963 triggered a chain of events that had profound effects on the PHS. Capitol Hill veteran Lyndon Johnson assumed the presidency and, bolstered by sympathy for the dead president and a landslide victory of his own in 1964, he embarked on a journey of legislative activism not seen since the early days of the New Deal. Johnson's extension of the New Frontier came to be called "The Great Society." Congress quickly passed landmark laws including the 1964 Economic Opportunity Act initiating the "War on Poverty" and, in 1965, Medicare and Medicaid, Model Cities, and the Voting Rights Act, as well as an avalanche of health-related legislation that covered issues from rat control to research facilities, from medical libraries to the training of nurse practitioners. Dr. Philip Lee was the assistant secretary for health and scientific affairs during this period.

I can remember...the President telling us directly that we should work to get as much legislation passed as we could....It was really 1965 to 1967, that two year period when the 89th Congress enacted more health legislation than all the previous Congresses put together....Things moved very, very quickly after January, 1965.[7]

Funding for biomedical research and for the NIH grew dramatically during the 1960s. President Lyndon Johnson paid his respects to both in a 1965 visit to the NIH campus. He is greeted (left to right) by Surgeon General William Stewart, NIH Director James Shannon, and Clinical Center Director Jack Masur. Dr. Stewart served as Surgeon General from 1965 to 1969.

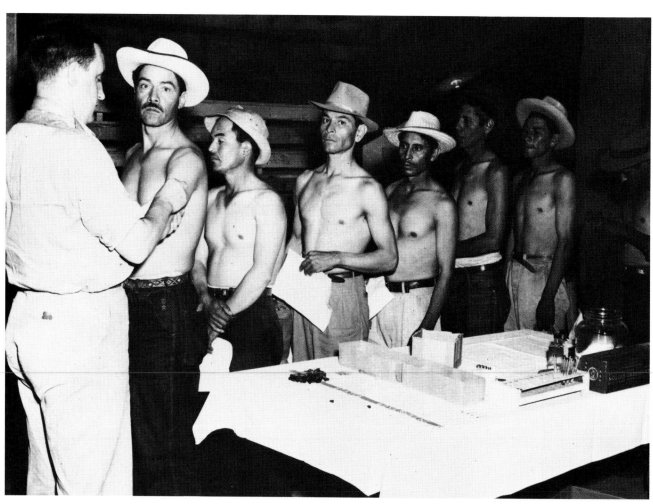

Between August and October of 1965 alone, Congress passed five major pieces of PHS legislation. These acts expanded the care given to migrant workers, extended the scope of federal vaccine assistance, funded a major campaign against measles, and introduced the concept of federally assisted health planning. The Health Research Facilities Amendments continued to build the NIH-based national research enterprise by providing $280 million for construction purposes. The Heart Disease, Cancer, and Stroke Amendments of 1965 were the result of the Debakey Commission, a presidential committee that had drafted a blueprint for a national attack on the great killers of the affluent society. This legislation established the Regional Medical Program (RMP), a network of medical centers funded to build bridges between medical research, medical education, and medical care. The RMP continued the federal emphasis on chronic disease research but it also sent a pragmatic message to the biomedical community, emphasizing the need to apply new knowledge to medical practice.

The PHS, however, was peripheral to several of the most important new health programs of this period. The Office of Economic Opportunity (OEO) quickly became involved in health through Head Start and the Job Corps. Most important in the long run, were the demonstration "Neighborhood Health Centers" first funded by the OEO in 1965. Different from the PHS grants-in-aid to health departments, the OEO model granted federal dollars directly to community organizations and combined health care with community development. Many political and community activists had come to see health departments as fragmented providers of service unresponsive to the needs of poor and minority communities. The OEO leapfrogged the PHS and their traditional health department partners, and funded groups new to the public health arena. The Neighborhood Health Center Program quickly won popular and congressional support, earning a $50 million appropriation in 1966 and opening fifty centers by 1968.[8]

For different reasons, Medicare and Medicaid also bypassed the PHS. To be sure, the debate about government assisted health care for the elderly had focused on proposed amendments to the Social Security Act rather than any modifications to the public health system. But since Parran's retirement in 1948 and Mountin's death in 1952, the PHS had been little involved in medical care policy, despite the growing importance of this issue in national policy debates. Many in the PHS saw Medicare itself as "an insurance company" and they felt that the PHS "was not in the check-writing business."[9] Congress and HEW agreed; when Medicare and its companion program for the care of the poor, Medicaid, became law in 1965, they were placed elsewhere in the department.

Water pollution control became an increasingly embattled area,

Newly legislated programs of the New Frontier and the Great Society aimed to provide services to the poor and the aged. Certain of them had particular importance for the PHS including the migrant health program (opposite below), Medicare (opposite above left), and neighborhood health centers set up in conjunction with community organizations (opposite above right).

with the environmental lobby continuing to criticize the PHS and pushing for a new agency of its own. Engineers within the Service felt caught between an ever more demanding public and a PHS leadership that was predominantly medical and, in their judgment, insufficiently interested in environmental issues. In 1961, all authority for water pollution control was transferred from the Surgeon General to the HEW secretary, and a 1965 law set up a Federal Water Pollution Control Administration that was promptly moved from HEW to the Department of the Interior. These events foreshadowed the creation of the Environmental Protection Agency in 1970 and the virtual eclipse of the PHS as the leader of the federal environmental movement.

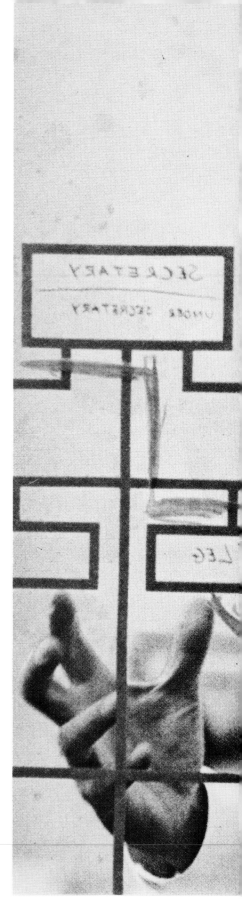

I n August of 1965, in the midst of this legislative high season, a bureaucracy shaker named John Gardner, the author of two books entitled *Excellence* and *Self-Renewal*, took over as HEW secretary. Six weeks later, Luther Terry retired as Surgeon General. Gardner named Heart Institute director, Dr. William Stewart, to replace him. A pediatrician, whose PHS career began in 1951 as an Epidemic Intelligence Service officer, Stewart had extensive health policy experience, having served on the staffs of both Surgeons General Burney and Terry as well as on that of previous HEW secretary, Anthony Celebrezze. Stewart came to office at an exciting and troubling moment in the history of the PHS. Federal health programs were growing at a staggering rate in and around the PHS. Notwithstanding the health programs that went elsewhere, the PHS budget virtually doubled between 1963 and 1968. The public stake in health was going up and, inevitably, this led to increased scrutiny of the PHS.

Secretary Gardner put it clearly in announcing Stewart's appointment:

> The President is deeply interested in the health activities of the Federal Government....Quite aside from the exacting standards set by the President there is reason for the Public Health Service to set its sights high. It stands at a critical point in its history. It will either take a leap forward, or it will become mired in its own internal conflicts and history will pass it by.[10]

The financial and political investment that the Johnson administration was making in health brought the structure and the ethos of the PHS, in general, and the Commissioned Corps, in particular, into question. "When times changed rapidly and the demands upon the Public Health Service ballooned far beyond anything that was earlier imaginable," wrote one critic, "the officer corps was caught without many of the talents it needed, but it was reluctant to assign high positions to persons outside the corps."[11] From 1870 until the mid-1960s, the leadership of the PHS consisted entirely of career commissioned

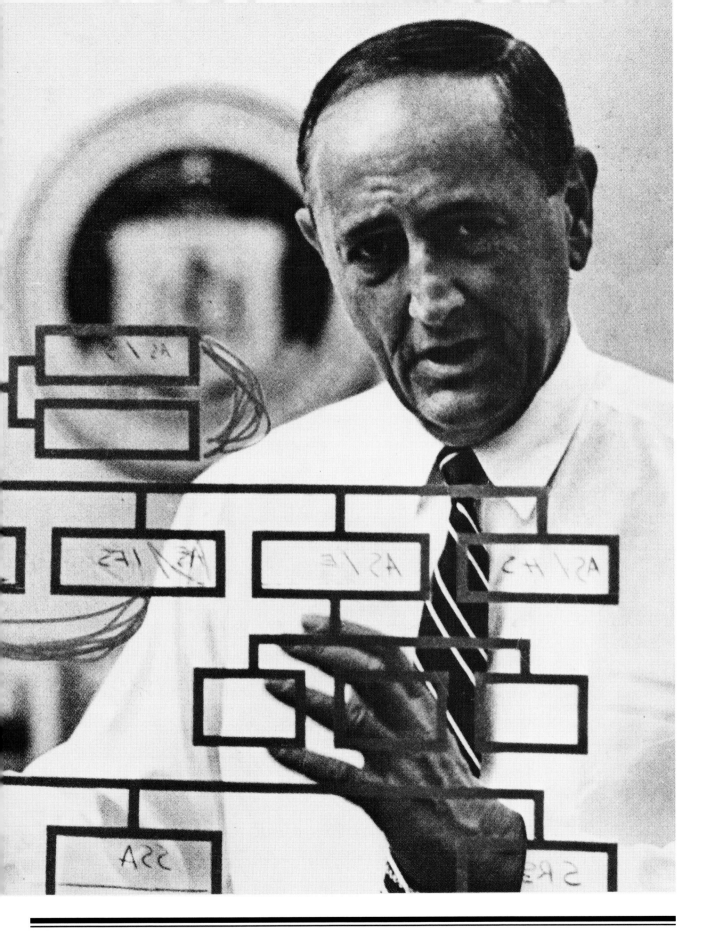

John Gardner (above), HEW secretary from 1965 to 1968, reorganizes his department. An advocate of institutional renewal, Gardner changed the leadership, content, and style of the PHS.

St. Elizabeths and the Legacy of Dorothea Dix

For many years, the name "St. Elizabeths" was synonymous with federal mental health activities. Although St. Elizabeths is not a PHS institution today nor was it at its inception, the hospital has been an important element of the mental health programs of the PHS and the nation as a whole for almost 150 years.

During the 1840s and 1850s, well-known humanitarian Dorothea Dix successfully lobbied more than twenty State legislatures to construct mental hospitals. In the same reformist spirit, she convinced Congress to pass a bill she had drafted appropriating funds for a "Government Hospital for the Insane." Ground was broken for the Government Hospital in 1852 on a magnificent, 300-acre site overlooking Washington, D.C. known as "the Saint Elizabeth's tract." The first building at the site was a "collegiate gothic" structure complete with battlements and buttresses called the Center Building. It was contructed of bricks made of soil from the tract and wood from trees in the surrounding forest. Opened in 1855, it contained wards, kitchens, a chapel, and an apartment for the superintendent. The first residents were fifty-three patients transferred from a Maryland asylum including "Patient Number 7" who, the records show, was a man who had attempted to assassinate President Andrew Jackson by firing two pistol shots at him at point-blank range. Both misfired.

In its early days, the hospital cared mainly for members of the Army and Navy and residents of the District of Columbia. During the Civil War the institution was used to house recuperating soldiers and a small factory for making artificial limbs was set up on the grounds. The soldiers did not wish to be stigmatized by writing to relatives that they were in an insane asylum so, instead, they just wrote that they were at St. Elizabeths Hospital. The name stuck and was offically changed in later years. It lost the apostrophe along the way and has remained without it ever since.

Dorothea Dix's legacy was humane treatment of the insane. Asylum—protection—was the idea she had championed. From the outset, therefore, St. Elizabeths was dedicated to offering the most benevolent and advanced treatments for its patients.

"Moral treatment"—the provision of congenial surroundings and the example of normal attendants—was the therapeutic philosophy of the early years of the hospital. This approach stood in marked contrast to the typically punitive treatments of the day and the frequent use of jails for the insane. Moral therapy emphasized education, healthful pursuits, kindliness, and a comfortable environment. A thousand trees of many different species from around the world were planted on the grounds by the employees to provide a beautiful environment for the patients. This approach also emphasized work and, as a result, patients were employed in a number of in-house industries.

During the 1880s and 1890s, more professionals and more advanced treatment methods were introduced at the hospital. A neuropathologist was hired, a nursing school was opened, and hypnotism and hydrotherapy were introduced. Indeed, St. Elizabeths was the first hospital in the United States to

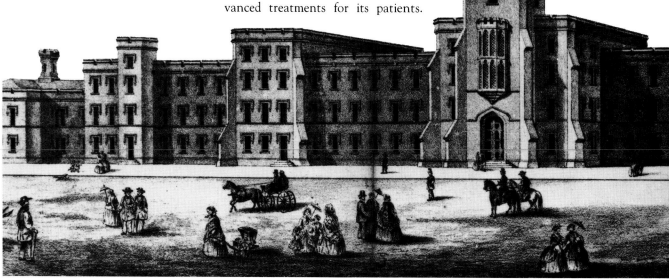

use the latter therapy. On summer days during this period, John Philip Sousa could be found at the hospital providing entertainment for the inmates. During these years, many of the 124 buildings that eventually dotted the site were built including residential halls, shops, and a bakery.

Over the years, various forms of psychotherapy, including milieu therapy, psychoanalysis, occupational therapy, group therapy, and dance therapy were introduced at the hospital. St. Elizabeths was also the first public hospital to use psychodrama as a method of treatment. In the 1950s, the hospital was the site of important psychopharmacological research with the sequential introduction of tranquilizers, antidepressants and antipsychotic agents. Innovation continued when, in 1957, Saint Elizabeths entered into a collaborative research program with the National Institute of Mental Health and created the Neuropharmacology Research Center. This was followed by the opening, in 1961, of the Behavioral and Clinical Studies Center at Saint Elizabeths.

From 1946 to 1958, the hospital was home to Ezra Pound, the noted American poet who had worked for the Ital-ians, broadcasting Fascist propaganda during the Second World War. At his subsequent trial for treason, he was found mentally unfit and was sent to St. Elizabeths where he lived in confinement. During the postwar period, the hospital census grew steadily reaching a high point of 5,500 patients in the 1950s. In the following decade, Saint Elizabeths was in the vanguard of the move to deinstitutionalize patients, and its inpatient numbers began to decrease quickly. The year 1967 was the last in which the hospital operated a coal-fed steam engine which ran on a one-mile track to bring tons of coal from the main railroad to heat the facilities.

The year 1967 also saw a major change in the administration of St. Elizabeths and its relationship to the PHS. Originally run by the Interior Department, the hospital, like the PHS, had moved to the Federal Security Administration and, in 1953, to HEW. In 1967, HEW Secretary John Gardner transferred St. Elizabeths to the National Institute of Mental Health of the Public Health Service. This move consolidated the management of federal mental health services and increased the opportunities for collaborative research at the facility. Under the author-ity of the NIMH, deinstitutionalization continued, with the hospital opening its first community mental health center in 1969. By 1978, the inpatient census had decreased to 2,200 while the hospital's community mental health centers had a census of 3,300.

In keeping with recent federal policy favoring the placement of service programs at the local level, and because most of St. Elizabeths current patients are residents of the District of Columbia, Congress passed an Act in 1984 transferring authority and responsibility for mental health services to the District. In October of 1987, much of the physical plant and most of the programs of St. Elizabeths were turned over to the government of the District of Columbia. The NIMH maintains an active research program on the campus and residual responsiblity for some of the land and buildings.

Today, St. Elizabeths is a hospital and a community mental health center dedicated to the treatment of the mentally ill residing in the nation's capital. It also remains a basic and clinical research center with ongoing studies focusing on schizophrenia and psychopharmacology conducted by NIMH personnel. Late in the 20th century, St. Elizabeths continues to uphold Dorothea Dix's tradition of humane and advanced treatment for the mentally ill.

An 1860s rendering of the Center Building at St. Elizabeths.

officers. Despite the fact that more than 80 percent of PHS employees were civilians, no member of the civil service had ever run a bureau in the PHS and the Service's only political appointee, the Surgeon General, was chosen from the ranks of career officers. While this safeguarded the professionalism of PHS, it created a system that in the minds of some, was not adequately responsive to the needs of the rapidly changing health sector nor to the policies of elected political officials. Other critics, including the Bureau of the Budget, simply felt that the old PHS had outlived its time and should be replaced by a modern, political bureaucracy staffed entirely by the civil service.

These criticisms of the PHS dovetailed with Gardner's appraisal of the department. Since its inception, HEW had been a holding company and the secretary planned to reorganize it and, in the process, gain control of its fiefdoms. On April 25, 1966, he issued a secretarial directive which transferred all the statutory authorities of the Surgeon General to the secretary, thereby giving the secretary the legal basis to restructure the PHS. The resulting reorganization, designed by Stewart in conjunction with Gardner, left the PHS intact with the Surgeon General in charge of an expanded five-bureau structure. It lasted for only fifteen months. "John Gardner was very impatient to get things done," recalls Lee. "He was a great believer in self-renewal at the individual level and at the institutional level....I think he didn't see that coming out of the reorganization that Bill (Stewart) had created."[12]

Although Gardner was its architect, the next reorganization was carried out in the spring of 1968 by his successor, Wilbur Cohen, and it did redefine the PHS. Balancing politics and professional continuity, Cohen put Lee in charge of the PHS and made the Surgeon General his deputy. A practicing internist from the Palo Alto Clinic, Lee originally came to Washington in 1963 to work for the Agency for International Development but switched to HEW in 1965 at the invitation of Cohen who drew on Lee's clinical background to help with the implementation of Medicare. Three agencies reported to Lee in the new structure—the NIH; the omnibus Health Services and Mental Health Administration (HSMHA), comprised of the old bureaus of State and Medical Services as well as the NIMH and a welter of new programs; and the Food and Drug Administration, which had previously reported separately to the secretary. For the first time in the history of the PHS, a noncareer official had become the nation's top health officer. The name "Public Health Service" was retained largely out of respect for its utility rather than from a belief that the future organization would bear much resemblance to that of the past.

Apologists and opponents alike assumed they were viewing the end of the PHS. Old-line commissioned officers, in particular, were bitter. A mere eight PHS hospitals remained and they were under continuous siege from the Bureau of the Budget. The 600-member

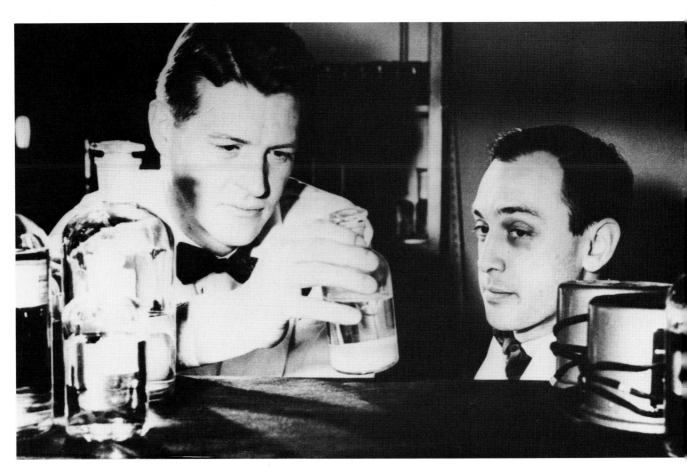

Four NIH intramural scientists have won Nobel prizes: Dr. Marshall Nirenberg (left below) in 1968 for translation of the genetic code and its function in protein synthesis; Dr. Julius Axelrod (below) in 1970 for his discoveries concerning transmitting substances in nerve terminals; Dr. Christian Anfinsen (left on left) in 1972 for contributions to the understanding of protein structure; and Dr. D. Carleton Gajdusek (right) in 1976 for demonstrating that kuru is a transmissible, "slow" virus infection.

Foreign Quarantine Division that maintained the tradition of guarding the nation's ports, was transferred to the CDC in 1967 and was reduced to a staff of sixty within several years. Many blamed Stewart for giving the PHS away and Lee for taking it. "(They) gave away the family jewels—the budget, program, everything. They wanted to run a tight little office and it did end up that way: neat, tight and little."[13] Lee and Stewart dealt with criticism on all sides. Their assessment of the needs of the country, the political realities that surrounded them, and the forceful presence of Secretaries Gardner and Cohen all argued absolutely for change. Stewart's view was that "the Commissioned Corps grew out of a strong cadre of people...(but it) was more identified with the way things were, and not the way things were going to be."[14] "Whenever you reorganize, you don't make any friends," observed Lee, noting that many people felt that he had "destroyed" the PHS because he was interested in medical care rather than public health.[15]

The relationship of the Commissioned Corps to the military came up regularly in deliberations about reorganization—especially as the war in Vietnam escalated. Stewart and Division of Nursing Director Margaret Arnstein visited Vietnam in 1966 and identified areas of civilian health and sanitation where the PHS could assist the government of South Vietnam. In subsequent years, a number of commissioned officers served temporary tours in Vietnam and six were assigned for extended duty. More difficult from a policy perspective, though, was the question of the military draft. Since the time of the Second World War, service in the Commissioned Corps had fulfilled an individual's draft obligation, a circumstance which had generally benefitted PHS recruitment. In the Vietnam era, many health professionals sought service in the Commissioned Corps, bringing many exceptional young scientists and practitioners, who might well not have been recruited in peacetime, to the NIH, the IHS, and elsewhere in the PHS. Although the Commissioned Corps could have been militarized by executive authority, neither Johnson nor Nixon chose to do so. In consequence, the Corps, like the National Guard, was never dispatched to Vietnam. The national service rendered by the Corps, as well as its availability for military or civilian emergencies, was sufficient to maintain its historic status as a uniformed service.

As it turned out, neither the PHS nor its Commissioned Corps was destined for extinction. Although the reorganization of the PHS and the "demotion" of the Surgeon General seemed draconian to some and long overdue to others, the PHS as a whole continued to thrive as measured by the steady growth of its budget, programs, and personnel. The PHS did

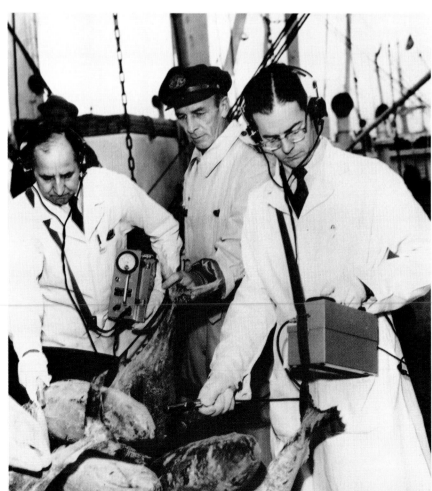

surrender some activities (water pollution) and missed out on others (Medicare and Medicaid) but it also gained a great deal that was new. The majority of PHS programs bustled along, working hard to perform the dozens of new jobs the Congress had given them. The topics appearing in the monthly publication, *PHS World*, give an idea of the nature and pace of the PHS enterprise of the time. The April, 1968 issue, for instance, covered Model Cities health programs in Baltimore, NIH support for infant mortality research, the workings of the National Center for Health Statistics, and a biographical sketch of Philip Lee. In the back there was an obituary of Thomas Parran. There was turnover in the PHS, to be sure, but there was also continuity and vigor.

Some agencies produced spectacular successes. With a Smallpox Surveillance Unit in place since 1962, the CDC took the lead for the PHS and the United States when, in 1967, the World Health Organization decided to attempt the eradication of smallpox. The CDC sent Dr. D. A. Henderson from Atlanta to Geneva to direct the Global Smallpox Eradication Program, and set to work on a regional and bilateral basis with twenty countries in Africa. A surveillance and containment strategy pioneered by Dr. William Foege proved extraordinarily effective and the African project was completed in 1970, ahead of schedule. The CDC also provided consultation for the smallpox eradication campaign in Brazil and helped to staff the massive programs in India and Bangladesh in the mid-1970s. In 1977, Dr. Jason Weisfeld of the CDC participated in the investigation of what proved to be the world's final case of smallpox in Merka, Somalia, which resulted in the ultimate declaration of "Smallpox Zero." More than 300 CDC staff took part in the smallpox fight, many of whom went on to leadership positions in national and international disease prevention work.[16]

These years saw the postwar investment in biomedical research pay rich dividends in scientific achievement, with Nobel honors being bestowed on several dozen investigators from around the world who had been supported by the NIH grant program. The first of four NIH scientists to win Nobel prizes for work done in this period was Marshall Nirenberg, who was recognized in 1968, for breaking the genetic code. Nirenberg was the first federal employee to win a Nobel prize since Theodore Roosevelt was awarded the Peace Prize in 1906. Julius Axelrod was honored in 1970 for work on the central nervous system neurotransmitter, norepinephrine. He demonstrated that norepinephrine was deactivated by "reuptake" as well as metabolic transformation, and that certain antidepressant drugs worked by blocking the reuptake mechanism. Christian Anfinsen received the prize in chemistry in 1972 for work elucidating the relationship of the amino acid sequence of proteins to their three dimensional structure. The 1976 prize in physiology or medicine went to Carleton Gajdusek for his

The Food and Drug Administration began as a food inspection program in the Department of Agriculture authorized by the Pure Food Act of 1906. Inspector John Earnshaw examines eggs (opposite above) in 1914 and, more recently, FDA scientists check fish for radioactivity (opposite below).

work showing that a "slow virus" that caused kuru, a fatal neurological disease found among the Fore people of New Guinea.

Achievements occurred in many spheres during this period. NIMH grew rapidly, opening 260 Community Mental Health Centers by 1968, and adding programs for the study of narcotics and alcohol to the agency's mental health thrust. Virological investigators Paul Parkman and Harry Meyer developed a rubella vaccine, Native American infant mortality continued a rapid decline, and PHS officers trained Peace Corps volunteers and served abroad with them. The CDC played its role in space exploration, designing and managing the National Aeronautics and Space Administration's quarantine program for the returning lunar astronauts.

Strength also came from programs added to the PHS. The new plan split up the Children's Bureau, finally putting the maternal and child health programs in the PHS—the idea that Surgeon General Wyman had spurned more than fifty years earlier. Additionally, the 1968 reorganization moved the Food and Drug Administration into the PHS. The FDA, like the Children's Bureau, had a proud and independent heritage dating from the Pure Food Act of 1906. Supported by a coalition of state and local food and drug officials, women's organizations, and muckraking journalists, that law gave consumers some protection against adulterated and mislabelled foods and drugs, and was seen at the time as a triumph for Progressive reform over the immoral forces of the unregulated marketplace. The intrepid director of the Department of Agriculture's Bureau of Chemistry, Harvey W. Wiley, was the Pure Food Act's principal booster, dramatizing the risks of the marketplace with his famous "poison squad"—a group of volunteer food testers. These men lived and dined together, eating foods that had been laced with measured amounts of additives such as benzoate of soda and formaldehyde, to determine the effects of chemicals on health. The hazards of life as a regulator were early demonstrated when, in 1912, Wiley resigned over the failure of the secretary of agriculture to back him in his struggle with the commercial interests he was attempting to police.

By 1933, a number of weaknesses in the 1906 law had become apparent and the FDA proposed major modifications to it. For five years the debate simmered with little public support for the FDA until 1937, when 107 people died from a preparation of the new "wonder drug," sulfanilamide, which had been adulterated with a solvent that proved to be toxic. The result was the much-toughened Food, Drug, and Cosmetic Act of 1938. Additional provisions were added to the law in subsequent years without, however, much in the way of additional resources. As late as 1960, the FDA remained a small operation. In televised hearings chaired by Senator Estes Kefauver, accumulated problems in new drug regulation called the agency's overall mission into question. This was further dramatized in 1962 by the work of Dr.

Starting in 1959, a marked increase in the number of infants born with severe deformities of the limbs called phocomelia (opposite) was noted in Europe and eventually linked to the use of thalidomide during pregnancy. Thalidomide was never marketed in the United States largely due to the stubborn skepticism of the FDA's Dr. Frances Kelsey, whose doubts delayed thalidomide's approval until its tragic effect had been realized. President Kennedy recognized Dr. Kelsey for her contribution in 1962 (above).

Frances Kelsey, an FDA scientist whose persistent skepticism kept the drug thalidomide from being marketed in the United States until its teratogenic effects were tragically discovered elsewhere. It was soon revealed that intense pressures to approve the drug had been brought to bear on both Kelsey and the agency. In the wake of the Kefauver hearings and the thalidomide episode, Congress increased its investment in the agency, tripling its staff and quintupling its budget between 1960 and 1970.

The FDA had always reported independently to the secretary. The importance of the FDA and its mission did not escape Gardner who envisioned a natural link between the FDA as a health agency and the broadened PHS he hoped to create. In 1966, he had appointed a commissioned officer, Dr. James Goddard, as the FDA commissioner and many felt that the PHS could help to improve professional recruitment and quality at the FDA. Putting the FDA in the PHS did not please traditionalists in either organization but made bureaucratic and strategic sense to the Gardner team. The wisdom of their decision would become apparent over the next decade as the FDA became an integral part of the PHS, adding traditional PHS responsibilities in radiation health and biologics control to its activities, and collaborating with the other agencies of the PHS in the areas of regulation, research, and surveillance.

The New Frontier, the Great Society, the Eighty-ninth Congress, Secretaries Gardner and Cohen, and the appetite of the American people for expanded health programs had, indeed, rocked the PHS. Although still not a national health department, the 1960s moved the PHS closer to that role by bringing it political leadership, expanding its scale and scope and, painfully, beginning to move it beyond its marine hospital heritage. True, the PHS failed to capture the enormous new federal medical care funding enterprise and it forfeited its environmental activities. Nevertheless, the "new" PHS carried forward the powerful NIH, maturing agencies such as the CDC (whose name was changed in 1970 from the Communicable Disease Center to the Center for Disease Control) and the NIMH, the newly acquired FDA, and a burgeoning set of health services and manpower programs. Despite criticism and controversy, the Commissioned Corps was very much alive, even as civil servants assumed leadership positions within the PHS.

The most profound problem with Gardner's reshaping of the PHS, as it turned out, was that neither he, nor his colleagues —Cohen, Stewart, or Lee—would be in office to see it through. Fitful and ill-disciplined as it appeared, Gardner's notion of institutional self-renewal had gone forward but it was far from complete when, in November of 1968, the nation elected Richard Nixon president. The impact of political turnover on the new leadership structure of the PHS would be tested immediately.

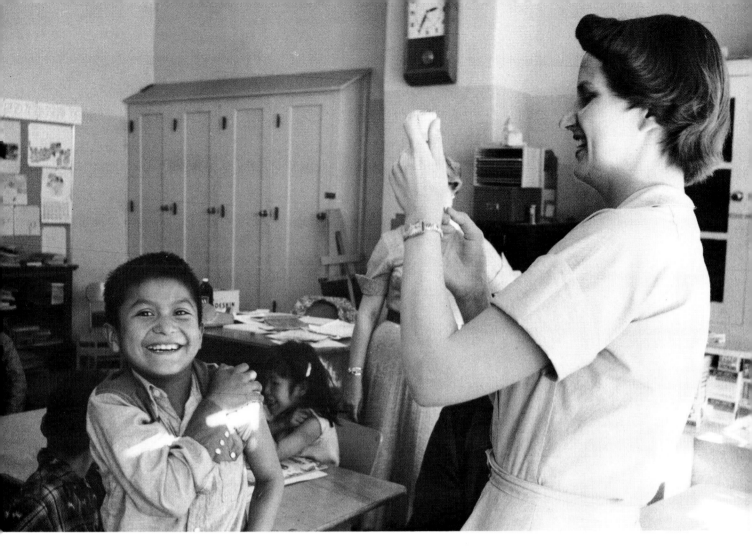

Care,
Cost,
And Prevention

"We spent a generation teaching (people) to go to the doctor early, and now we're telling them not to go at all."

THEODORE COOPER, M.D.

A lthough Richard Nixon came to the presidency preoccupied with international issues, he did have fixed domestic policy ambitions as well. He campaigned on a "law and order" platform, mistrusted federal solutions to social problems, and drew his greatest support from middle-class, middle-aged, white voters—his "silent majority"—most of whom were not partisans of the New Frontier and the Great Society. The rapid scuttling of these programs that was predicted by many, however, did not occur. A number of the new programs such as Head Start and the Neighborhood Health Centers were popular successes, while others, such as Medicare and health manpower grants, did benefit broad, and often conservative constituencies. Medicaid expanded access of the poor to the medical system, a goal still held in esteem by the majority in Congress.

The demand for health programs remained brisk—more medical schools, more neighborhood health centers, more Medicare—and contributed to a rapid increase in the public investment in health as well as a significant inflation in health care costs. It was not ideology or popularity so much as economics that came to challenge the programs of the PHS. The results of the guns and butter policies of the 1960s were inflation and unemployment in the 1970s, complicated by oil embargoes, trade deficits, and the devaluation of the dollar. It was inflation, in particular, that plagued the health sector. The period from 1969 to 1980 would be one of contradictory stresses for the PHS as it worked to sort out its new organization, pinioned between the public demand for more services and the increasingly urgent need to contain escalating health costs.

Selecting leadership for the PHS proved to be a problem for the new administration. Secretary of HEW, Robert Finch, chose Dr. John Knowles of the Massachusetts General Hospital for the position of assistant secretary for health but was blocked by strong conservative opposition, leaving the reorganization in limbo. In July of 1969, Finch appointed Dr. Roger Egeberg, dean of the University of Southern California School of Medicine, former director of the Los Angeles County General Hospital and physician to Douglas MacArthur during the Second World War, as assistant secretary for health. Egeberg recruited a colleague and a former member of his faculty, Dr. Jesse Steinfeld, to assist him with his new job. Steinfeld had served on the oncology staff at the NIH Clinical Center from its inception in 1953

The provision of medical care has been an important part of the work of the PHS in every epoch. Senior Assistant Surgeon Nancy Campbell from the Seattle PHS Hospital (opposite) on temporary assignment to Fort Chaffee, Arkansas examines a refugee from Cuba who arrived in the United States in the Mariel Boatlift of 1980.

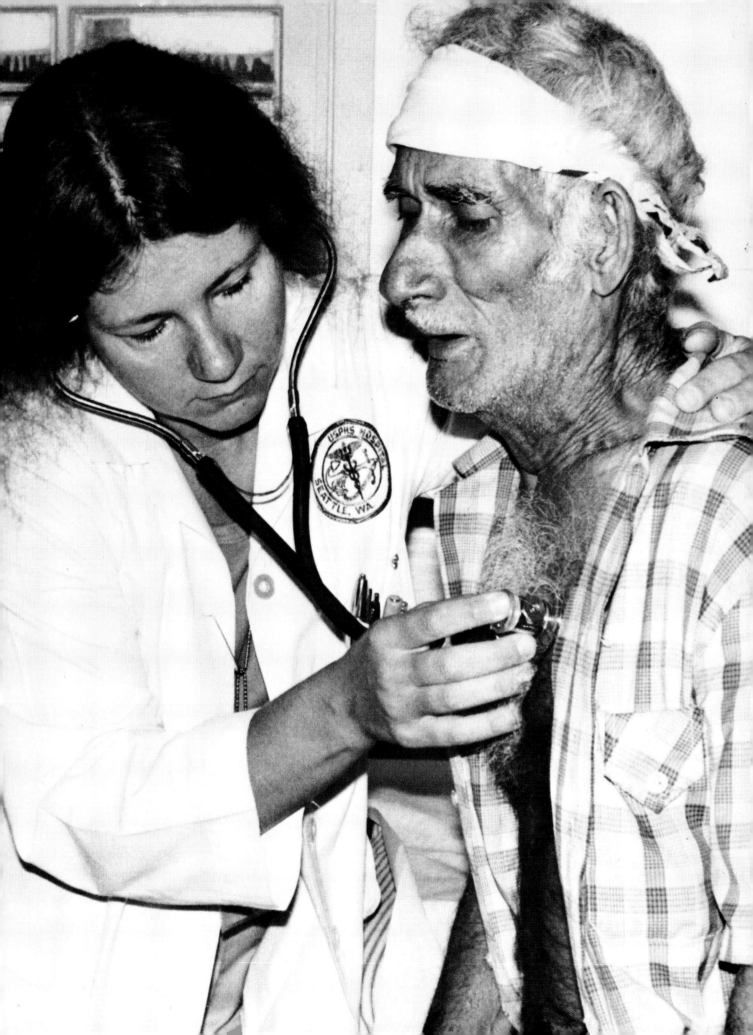

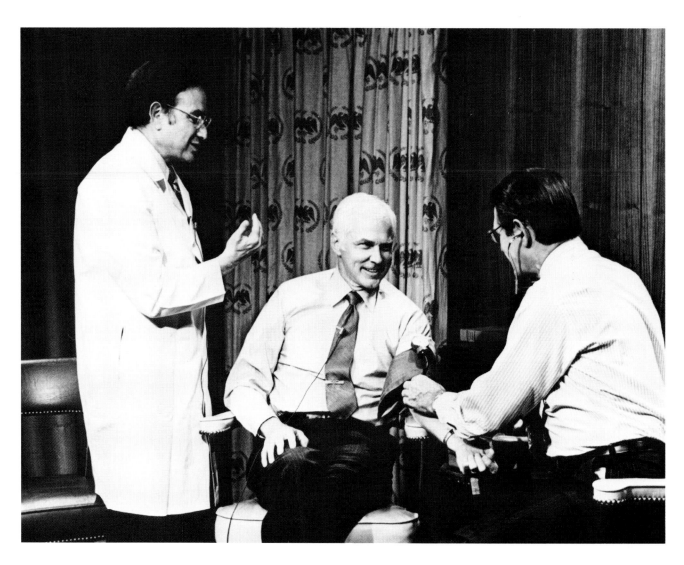

until 1958, when he moved to academic oncology in Los Angeles. In 1968, he returned to the NCI as deputy director. In December of 1969, over the protests of some advisors who thought the job should be left vacant, Finch appointed Steinfeld Surgeon General.

The signals were elaborately mixed. Egeberg was technically in charge, but the reorganization of 1968 had left his office with almost no staff to manage the PHS and, in consequence, PHS agency heads tended to work directly with the secretary or his staff. Steinfeld retained the tradition of authority but had little real power. His plight was compounded by the increasingly explicit campaign within the department and the Nixon White House to do away with the Commissioned Corps. Finch was replaced by Elliot Richardson, who appointed a former undersecretary of the department, John A. Perkins, to chair a committee on the future of the Commissioned Corps. Perkins' 1971 report concluded that the Corps was obsolete, relied too heavily on the military draft to attract personnel, and should be replaced by "a unified career system...within the civil service framework." The position of Surgeon General "tends to be confusing and leads to misunderstanding," it stated, adding that "sooner or later, symbolic values have to correspond to program and organizational realities....Our legislative recommendations would, if approved, in time abolish both the rank and the title."[1] The following week, the authoritative newsletter *Health and Medicine* wrote an early obituary of the Corps, reporting that "Very little doubt remains about the forthcoming fate of the PHS Commissioned Corps, its Surgeon General and the PHS hospital system....The report is expected to be implemented."[2]

The report was not implemented. Steinfeld spoke on behalf of internal opposition, asking in a memo that all commissioned officers respond through him to the secretary because "the report is so destructive to the Corps that we will continue to suffer damage to morale, to recruitment, and to retention...."[3] Richardson received complaints from many quarters including key members of Congress. Paul Rogers, the chairman of the House Subcommittee on Health, weighed in heavily for the Corps. "Paul Rogers wanted none of this nonsense in terms of doing away with the Surgeon General . . ." according to Dr. Merlin DuVal who replaced Egeberg as assistant secretary in July of 1971 at the same time as the Perkins Report was issued. "(He) did tell me at that time, 'Monte, don't get too fancy with this. We'll give you a lot of trouble on the Hill.'"[4]

Richardson backed away from any implementation of the Perkins report, frustrating but by no means declawing, the Corps' critics. At the beginning of the second Nixon administration, Steinfeld resigned, and Caspar Weinberger, who replaced Richardson as secretary, chose not to fill the position. Dr. Paul Ehrlich, the Deputy Surgeon General, carried out ceremonial functions, but the future of the Corps was in administrative escrow.

PHS leadership changed frequently during the Nixon administrations. The President (opposite below right) visited with (left to right) outgoing HEW Assistant Secretary Philip Lee, Surgeon General William Stewart, and new HEW Secretary Robert Finch in 1969. Dr. Jesse Steinfeld (above) served as Surgeon General from 1969 to 1973 and Dr. S. Paul Ehrlich, Jr. (opposite below left) as Acting Surgeon General from 1973 to 1977. National Heart Institute Director (and future Assistant Secretary for Health) Theodore Cooper (standing opposite above) and Assistant Secretary for Health Merlin DuVal (center) instruct HEW Secretary Elliot Richardson in blood pressure measurement.

Since 1914, the PHS has had a designated office involved with the health and safety of the industrial worker (opposite and above). The office, under various names, investigated work hazards of every sort including mercury poisoning among fur cutters in the hat industry; silicoses from granite, cement, textile, and mining work; and the toxicology of industrial chemicals. Legislation in 1970 established the National Institute of Occupational Safety and Health in the PHS with a primary mission of research and training in the field of occupational health.

The earthquake of PHS reorganization in the 1960s produced a series of aftershocks in the 1970s that consolidated a new structure for the PHS which with minor alterations, remains in place today. In 1970, President Nixon capped more than two decades of continued public concern about the deteriorating quality of the environment by creating the Environmental Protection Agency (EPA). The EPA merged most federal environmental activities, taking from the PHS programs in air pollution, solid waste, pesticides, drinking water, and some aspects of radiological health. Many of the environmental scientists and engineers who were commissioned officers in these programs moved to the new agency but remained on loan from the PHS — an arrangement that has continued to the present. The transfer of the core of federal environmental activities out of the government's principal health agency led to similar moves on the part of many state governments, weakening the linkages between human disease and the environment while accentuating the potential regulatory role of government in regard to the environment.

The passage of legislation in 1970 creating both the National Institute of Occupational Safety and Health (NIOSH) in the PHS and the Occupational Safety and Health Administration (OSHA) in the Department of Labor represented the culmination of decades of federal involvement in industrial hygiene. The PHS had been active in the area since 1910, when Surgeon General Wyman assigned a medical officer to the new federal Bureau of Mines to study diseases and injuries of miners. In 1914, the PHS established an Office of Industrial Hygiene and Sanitation which, under an evolving series of names, affiliated at first with the Hygienic Laboratory and the NIH and, later, with the Bureau of State Services, grew steadily in size and scope. The unit investigated work hazards of every sort including oral cancer in radium dial painters (who licked their brushes); mercury poisoning among fur cutters in the hat industry; silicoses from granite, cement, textile, and mining work; and the toxicology of industrial chemicals. Studies were done on workers in the granite cutting industry in Vermont whose high rates of pulmonary tuberculosis were dramatically reduced by stringent dust control measures. Scientists in the program pioneered the use of epidemiological assessment at work sites and developed the important concept of tolerance limits to hazardous exposures.

Starting in the 1930s, the PHS assisted state health departments in developing occupational health programs which, by the 1950s, were widespread. These programs were far from standardized, and organized labor, concerned about the unevenness of state laws, began a long campaign to "federalize" occupational health in the belief that uniform national standards would upgrade worker protection. The result was the 1970 law creating NIOSH and OSHA. Although the

Oral cancers were common among
radium watch dial painters (above) who
licked their brushes to improve the
points. In 1929, Dr. L. R. Thompson of
the PHS led a team of scientists who
investigated the health effects of radium
which included an examination of every
watch dial painter in the United States
and led to major changes in industry
practice.

principal missions of NIOSH are research and training (as opposed to OSHA whose job is enforcement), the right of entry into work places and the mandate to recommend safety standards for workers came with the new law and has made NIOSH both active and controversial. Housed at the CDC, the agency grew rapidly during the 1970s, only to suffer cutbacks in its budget and programs during the Reagan administration.[5]

The largest aftershock of the earlier PHS reorganization, however, came not as an addition or deletion of activities but as a major settling out. In 1972, the PHS consisted of three agencies—the newly arrived FDA, the evergrowing and quasi-independent NIH, and the huge administrative vessel into which the rest of the PHS had been poured, the Health Services and Mental Health Administration. Called "Hart, Schaffner and Marx" by some, HSMHA included the Indian Health Service and the National Center for Health Statistics, the CDC and the Regional Medical Program, the PHS hospitals and health planning program, and more. When Secretary Richardson brought in DuVal as assistant secretary for health, he charged him with getting hold of the PHS and managing it as a "line" officer. DuVal and his successor, Dr. Charles Edwards, did precisely that during 1972 and 1973, building the staff and competence of their office, dismantling HSMHA, and realigning the PHS in a six-agency structure. To the FDA and the NIH were added four new agencies spawned by HSMHA—the CDC on its own; the Health Services Administration (HSA), comprised of PHS health delivery activities; the Health Resources Administration (HRA), made up of training, facilities and construction programs; and the Alcohol, Drug Abuse and Mental Health Administration (ADAMHA).[6]

The continued growth of federal attention to the arena of behavioral health was signaled by the creation of ADAMHA. Iowa Senator Harold Hughes, a recovering alcoholic and former truck driver, led a campaign to stimulate public awareness of alcohol as a major health problem. The result was a law passed in 1970 that established the National Institute on Alcohol Abuse and Alcoholism (NIAAA) within NIMH. Continued concern about drug addiction led to legislation dedicating more money to community-based prevention and treatment programs and to the formation in 1972 of the National Institute on Drug Abuse (NIDA) also within NIMH. As a result of the formal emphasis thus given to alcohol and drug abuse, ADAMHA emerged from the 1973 reorganization as a behavioral health superagency, with NIAAA and NIDA taking their places beside NIMH in the new organization. The new laws as well as previous NIMH legislation gave strong emphasis to community programs, making the three institutes hybrids of service and research and resulting in their placement outside of NIH—a controversial decision that would be revisited regularly in the ensuing years.

The reorganization of 1973 represented the effective digestion of the legislation of the previous decade by the PHS and resulted in a period of relative calm in administrative matters. Fiscal, political, and clinical problems, though, arrived at the door of the PHS with exceptional regularity through the mid-1970s. Government health costs grew at roughly 20 percent a year during this period, with inflation in medical services moving well ahead of general inflation. Although a major stimulant to both these phenomena was the Medicare program, it fell to the PHS to undertake what became known generically as "cost containment."

Struggles between free marketeers and regulators, doctors and economists, and politicians and bureaucrats led to a variety of cost containment strategies that the PHS managed. Nixon introduced the health maintenance organization (HMO) as "a new national health strategy" in a speech in 1971. Legislation passed in 1973 set up an HMO program and the PHS began making grants and loans to stimulate the formation of HMOs. After much debate, legislation establishing Professional Standards Review Organizations (PSRO) to review the use of Medicare by physicians was enacted in 1973. The health planning law was amended in 1974 to provide funding for an elaborate network of state agencies intended to slow the construction of unnecessary health facilities.

Cost containment was hard work, had little impact on the continued escalation of medical costs, and tended to create political controversy everywhere. Dr. Theodore Cooper, a cardiac surgeon and National Heart Institute director, who succeeded Charles Edwards as the assistant secretary for health in 1975, captured the human side of the cost containment conundrum.

> It's a combination of human nature and a miscalculation of how people react to benefits. On the one hand, you're telling them to go early, get all these things. Then you tell them, on the other hand, "But don't use the system." We have not been terribly effective in conveying to the public what it is we're talking about. We spent a generation teaching them to go to the doctor early, and now we're telling them not to go at all.[7]

Unlike the amorphous challenge of cost containment, the public's discovery of the Tuskegee syphilis project in 1972 created a specific clinical and ethical crisis for the PHS. Begun forty years earlier by the Venereal Disease Division in conjunction with the Tuskegee Institute and the Macon County (Alabama) Health Department, the project followed the long-term, clinical course of a group of black men with advanced, untreated syphilis. The discovery of the effectiveness of penicillin against syphilis in the 1940s did not alter the course of the project that kept careful track of its untreated subjects, providing them with free medical care for other ailments while attempting to obtain autopsies at the time of their deaths. Although findings from the study had been published in the medical literature from time to

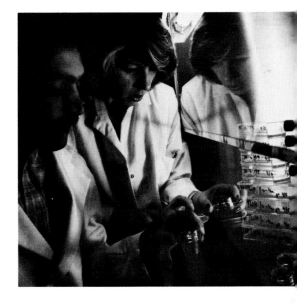

The Alcohol, Drug Abuse and Mental Health Administration was created in 1973, consolidating PHS research and treatment programs for mental and addictive disorders. Research in the neurosciences (above) aims to produce new knowledge for the prevention and treatment of problems such as chronic mental illness, depression, and alcoholism (opposite).

PHS physician Stuart Mackler examines a Vietnamese boy in 1967. Mackler was serving on the Coast Guard cutter Yakutat *and regularly held sick call in Vietnamese coastal villages. A number of PHS officers served temporary tours in Vietnam and six did extended duty working with civilian populations.*

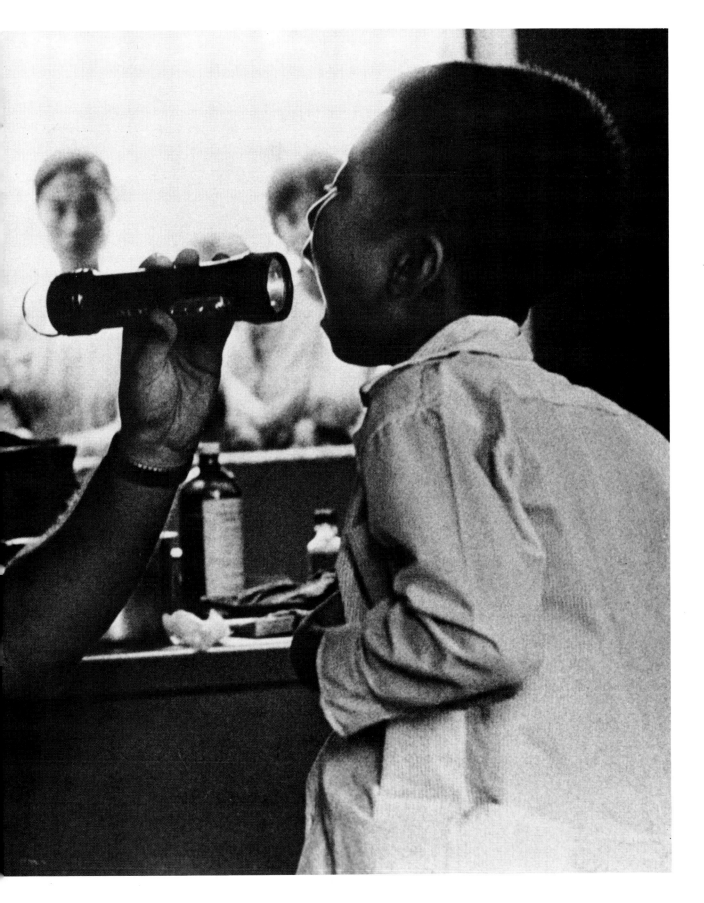

181

time, it was Peter Buxton, a CDC venereal disease program worker in the mid-1960s, who began to raise questions about its rationale and ethics—questions that were dismissed by the CDC leadership as unfounded. At length, Buxton went to the press where the story exploded, calling into question the medical ethics, racial attitudes, and scientific judgment of the PHS.

The CDC defended its previous decision to continue the project on the grounds that penicillin treatment of advanced syphilis had led to adverse reactions in some patients, a judgment that was not accepted by an outside panel quickly convened to review the forty-year experiment. The panel called for an immediate termination of the study, asked for free medical care for the living participants, and found the government guidelines for protecting human experimental subjects to be woefully inadequate. A $10 million, out-of-court settlement provided some recompense for the survivors and the families of deceased participants, and public reaction to the episode, as well as Senate hearings on it, contributed to greatly tightened controls on human experimentation. For the PHS, the Tuskegee Project ended as a painful reminder that the practices of the past are not always applicable—let alone ethical—in the present.[8]

Tactics, not ethics, were key to the swine flu campaign. A virus, isolated in January 1976 from four sick Army recruits, preoccupied the PHS and the nation for most of that year. Dubbed "swine flu" and thought to be similar to the organism responsible for the 1918 pandemic, it raised the question of the feasibility and advisability of a universal immunization campaign on a crash basis. By March, the CDC and the PHS, backed by a panel of experts, had made that recommendation to President Ford who, flanked by Drs. Sabin and Salk, announced his request to Congress for a $135 million emergency appropriation for the preparation of a swine flu vaccine to be ready for mass use by the fall. Congress approved the funds and the CDC directed the development and production of the vaccine.

Many concluded that the swine flu had arrived in August when 221 people in Pennsylvania came down with severe respiratory illness, 34 of them eventually dying. The EIS team that investigated the outbreak rapidly narrowed the source of the epidemic to the Bellevue-Stratford Hotel in Philadelphia where the preponderance of those infected had attended an American Legion convention in the preceding week. Further work proved that the agent in "Legionnaires' disease" was not the swine flu. Six months later, in January of 1977, CDC scientists Charles Shepard and Joseph McDade identified a previously unrecognized bacterium, *Legionella pneumophilia*, as the cause of Legionnaires' disease.

In the meantime, on October first, the swine flu inoculation campaign began in earnest. In the ensuing ten weeks, almost fifty million Americans were vaccinated—an unprecedented accomplish-

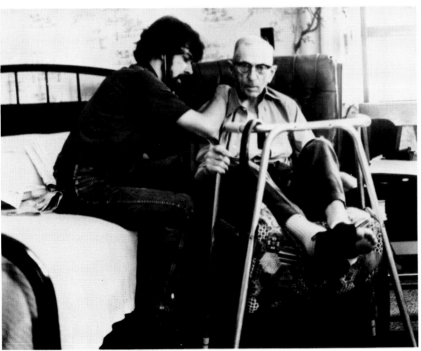

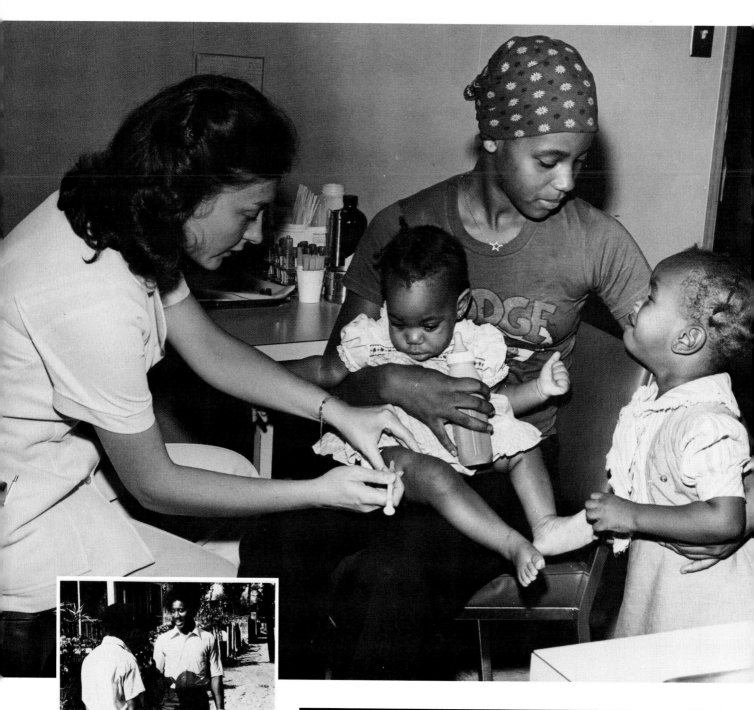

The Service delivery activities as well as the recruitment strategies of the PHS in the mid-1970s emphasized community health programs. Dr. Fred Stallings (left) worked for the National Health Service Corps in Atlanta and doubled as a recruiter for the program. Starting in 1977 and working through local health departments and community health centers, the CDC sponsored a nationwide campaign to improve the declining immunization levels in children (above).

ment, testifying to cooperation between government, industry, and the populace as a whole. In late November, however, cases of a rare, paralytic condition known as Guillain-Barre Syndrome were reported, first from Minnesota and Alabama, and then from elsewhere. By mid-December it was clear that, though the numbers were small, a causal relationship existed between the vaccine and the paralysis. Moreover, there had not been a single report of swine flu in the United States since the four cases of the previous winter. On December 16, 1976, with the concurrence of President Ford, Assistant Secretary Cooper announced the suspension of the vaccination campaign. At some cost but with considerable skill, the PHS had led the United States through an exercise in self-defense against an epidemic that never arrived.[9]

When Jimmy Carter was elected president, he chose the activist political administrator, Joseph Califano, as HEW secretary who, in turn, reached back to his Johnson administration roots to appoint Dr. Julius Richmond as assistant secretary for health. Pediatrician, academician, and child mental health advocate, Richmond had served with distinction as the founding director of Project Head Start and played an important role in the OEO health programs of the mid-1960s. Richmond agreed to return to Washington from his position at Harvard, provided he could serve as Surgeon General as well as assistant secretary. This formula avoided the ambiguities of twin PHS leaders and provided tacit support for the Commissioned Corps concept by the new administration. Califano accepted and Richmond went to work.

High on Richmond's agenda was what he called "health equity"—access to health care for traditionally disadvantaged Americans. He, in fact, took over a PHS that had become heavily involved in carrying out exactly that mission. Despite the intentions of the Nixon-Ford administration to limit domestic programs and restrain health care expenditures, the primary health care programs of the PHS had grown rapidly through the first half of the decade bolstered by evident need and congressional support. Medicaid had provided a form of health insurance to the most destitute, but many rural and poorer urban communities remained unable to recruit or retain physicians. Between 1970 and 1973, the OEO Neighborhood Health Centers were transferred to the PHS Health Services Administration as Community Health Centers (CHC) where many thought they were slated for extinction. Although the transfer did result in a shift from the all-purpose health center toward a more limited medical model of practice, their numbers grew from 157 in 1974 to 872 in 1980, and included special programs for the Appalachia region and for migrants. CHC funding maintained its OEO, community-action roots, with

Four cases of swine flu in military recruits at Fort Dix, New Jersey in the winter of 1976 precipitated a rapid national effort to develop, produce, and distribute a vaccine by the following fall. Borough President Robert Conner (above, seated) receives the first swine flu injection on Staten Island in October, 1976 from PHS nurse Jerrilynn Regan flanked by Andrew Passeri and Dr. Florence Kaveler. Debate about the strategy persisted and the failure of the epidemic of swine flu to materialize combined with the occurrence of Guillain-Barre syndrome in vaccine recipients brought about the cancellation of the campaign in December of 1976.

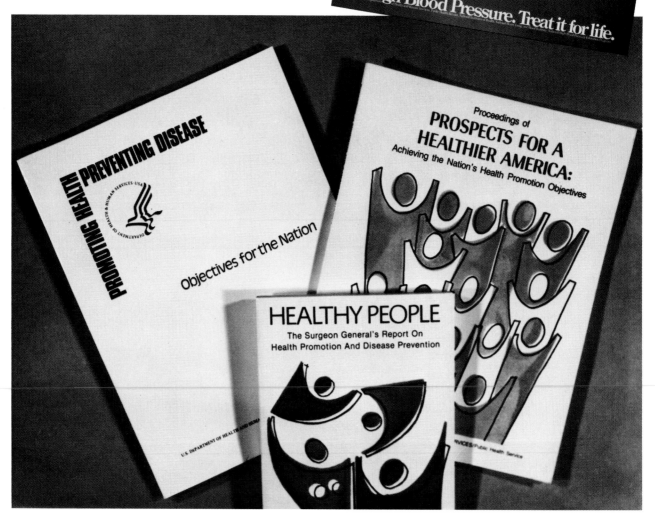

the grants being made directly to community corporations that only rarely involved local health departments.[10]

More unorthodox than this was a program called the National Health Service Corps (NHSC), proposed originally in 1969 by a young physician named Laurence Platt who joined the PHS to serve his draft obligation. The NHSC quickly found its way into law, fulfilling Platt's vision. "The Corps would be a mechanism," he wrote in the clear voice of his times,

> by which the "Establishment" could provide individuals with the opportunity to serve a social need pertinent to today's complex problems and demands. And it would demonstrate an interest on the part of government in those problems and demands—a demonstration sorely needed.[11]

The NHSC sent physicians, dentists, nurse practitioners, and physician's assistants to clinical placements in health manpower shortage areas. In the process, the PHS assumed responsibility for the care of the general public (as opposed to sailors or prisoners or Indians) for the first time in its history. In remodeled trailers in small towns and in urban store fronts, as well as in more conventional offices, the NHSC went to work providing services to poor and isolated Americans. The program was given a boost in 1972 when a scholarship provision was added to the law that enabled the PHS to pay for health professional schooling in return for a year-for-year commitment to serve in the NHSC. By 1980, the NHSC had 2,080 providers in the field and was supporting the education of 6,000 more health science students still in school. Richmond, with Califano's backing, was a strong advocate of the coordinated use of PHS resources in disadvantaged communities. In this spirit, NHSC professionals were placed in conjunction with grants from the Community Health Center, Migrant Health, and Maternal and Child Health Programs to build complete health systems—a strategy that governed PHS program development during these years.

T he push for equity in access to health services during the Carter administration was matched by a rejuvenated interest in an old PHS theme—disease prevention. Governed by this principle, the sanitary reform movement of the late 19th and early 20th centuries had helped to control the worst depredations of contagious disease in the United States, contributing to enormous improvements in the longevity of the population. Frequently called the "Public Health Revolution," it targeted acute infectious illness, leaving cardiovascular disease and cancer as the prevailing killers of the late 20th century. Richmond conceived a "Second Public Health Revolution" that would tackle the agents of contemporary mortality—smoking, drinking, diet, sedentary living, and poor safety

Dr. Julius Richmond served both as Surgeon General and as assistant secretary for health from 1976 to 1981. A strong advocate of preventive medicine, he poses (opposite above left, at right) with consumer representative Virginia Knauer and Deputy Surgeon General John Greene. He sponsored the publication of Healthy People (below), the "bible" of the health promotion and disease prevention movement. All agencies of the PHS including the National Heart, Lung, and Blood Institute (opposite above right) increased their health promotion activities.

Viral Hemorrhagic Fevers

Patients with Marburg fever were treated in this isolation unit in the mid-1970s.

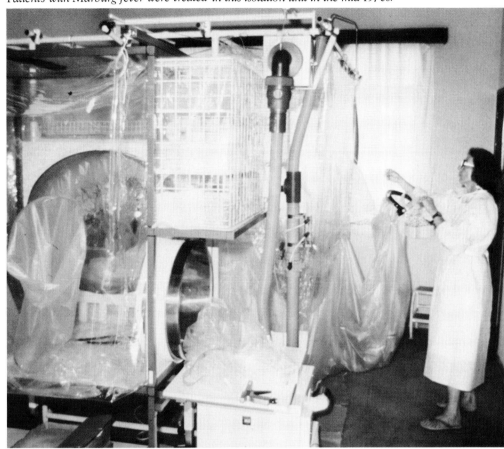

In 1967 in Marburg, West Germany, a new and frightening "hemorrhagic fever" appeared in epidemic form among laboratory workers exposed to tissues of imported African green monkeys. Within a decade, two other new viral hemorrhagic fevers would emerge from the African forest. Yellow fever, long the object of PHS prevention and control campaigns, is the world's best known hemorrhagic fever. The newly recognized diseases, Marburg, Ebola, and Lassa fevers, became the subject of intensive epidemiological and virological research at the Centers for Disease Control. The three shared a number of characteristics: the capacity for person-to-person transmission; severe and often lethal infection characterized by terminal shock and hemorrhage; a high degree of hazard in laboratory and hospital settings; the risk of introduction into the United States by infected travellers; and unknown virus reservoirs in nature, and vectors to man.

Centers for Disease Control epidemiologists have investigated epidemics of Marburg, Lassa, and Ebola fevers in Africa, often facing great hardships and personal risk of contagion. Until 1972, Lassa fever was known only as a disease transmitted from person to person in hospital outbreaks. In that year, CDC scientists described a community-based epidemic in Sierra Leone and Dr. Thomas Monath identified the rodent species harboring the virus. In 1976, a CDC field station in Sierra Leone under the direction of Dr. Joseph McCormick began a remarkable series of investigations that would prove Lassa fever to be a leading cause of morbidity and mortality in West Africa. This work would also define the risk factors and the clinical spectrum of the disease and

demonstrate the efficacy of early treatment with the antiviral agent, ribavarin. Just as the field station in Sierra Leone began operations, a particularly terrifying outbreak struck southern Sudan and northern Zaire. An international team led by Dr. Karl Johnson of the CDC investigated the outbreak in Zaire, which caused death in 280 of its 318 victims—an 88 percent mortality rate, second only to that of rabies. Application of the principles of isolation and disinfection halted the outbreak, and the use of protective gear prevented contamination of the investigators. Ebola, the virus that caused this epidemic, was isolated at the CDC and shown to be a relative of the Marburg agent.

Safe conditions for study of these highly hazardous viruses require sophisticated methods for complete separation of infectious material from the lab-

oratory worker, using sealed cabinets with glove-ports or space suits. The initial isolation of Marburg virus from clinical specimens was conducted under less than ideal conditions in a laboratory trailer loaned by the National Cancer Institute to the CDC. The first permanent laboratory was opened in 1969—the year Lassa fever was discovered. In 1988, after several intermediate stops, the maximum containment laboratory was moved to a state-of-the-art, third-generation, biocontainment facility in the new virology building on the CDC's Atlanta campus. The focus of current research is on the development of improved diagnostic methods and genetically engineered vaccines. Though a fuller understanding of Lassa, Ebola, and Marburg fevers is emerging, they remain as ominous reminders of the potential for new plagues in any epoch.

189

Under the auspices of the Agency for International Development, PHS pharmacist James Moore (above far left, in uniform) went to Guatemala to provide assistance after the 1976 earthquake. The PHS sent teams abroad following natural disasters in Africa, Asia, and Central America and provided medical triage and care for hundreds of thousands of Southeast Asian, Cuban, and Haitian refugees arriving in the United States during the period from 1975 to 1980.

practices. Toward this end, he appointed Dr. J. Michael McGinnis to head an Office of Disease Prevention and Health Promotion and produce a document that would inaugurate this new movement.

McGinnis produced two volumes. If *Healthy People*, the first, was the bible of the movement, the second, *Objectives for the Nation*, was to be its manual. Published in 1979 as "The Surgeon General's Report on Health Promotion and Disease Prevention," *Healthy People* set forth ambitious goals for the year 1990 that included a 35 percent decrease in infant mortality, a 20 to 25 percent decrease in mortality in other age groups and a 20 percent reduction in the number of days of illness among the elderly. Califano put it simply in his forward to the report: "You, the individual, can do more for your own health and well-being than any doctor, any hospital, any drug, any exotic medical device."[12] The campaign appealed to prudence and logic. It also appealed to the growing forces advocating cost containment who saw the role of government in health promotion and disease prevention as a low-cost catalytic activity.

The process itself was not easy. "People were jumpy," recalled Richmond. "While we had eradicated smallpox around the world, we hadn't yet eradicated measles from this country, and they were very sensitive to the complexities of doing it well."[13] Nonetheless, using an extensive network of medical, behavioral, and public health consultants, the PHS developed a series of specific targets within set categories for each age-group that were compiled and published in 1980 as *Objectives for the Nation*. The CDC, long the keeper of the disease prevention tradition within the PHS, increased its efforts in health promotion and education. The NIH, often protective of its prerogatives in basic research, appointed an associate director for prevention. Many states adapted the national goals to their own needs and set about campaigns to increase public awareness and participation. *Healthy People*, the book, and healthy people, the concept, provided the backdrop for a stirring of national consciousness about lifestyle that has resulted in changes in personal habits, medical practice, and commercial activities, as well as in public programs. The Second Public Health Revolution is ongoing.

The robustness of the U.S. population that was the object of this campaign, however, stood in contrast to the condition of the many refugee populations with whom the PHS worked during this period. The CDC, in particular, provided epidemiological assistance and health needs assessments in Nigeria during the 1967-70 civil war; in natural disasters in Peru, East Pakistan, Nicaragua, and Guatemala between 1970 and 1976; and in the Sahelian countries of Africa during the 1973-75 famine years. The largest refugee programs of the PHS, though, were the result of political rather than natural calamities and took place within the United States. In the aftermath of the fall of Saigon in 1975, hundreds of thousands of refugees from Vietnam, Cambodia, and Laos were accepted for resettlement. Continued turmoil in the region led to a steady exodus and, at the high point in 1979, almost 15,000 Southeast Asians were arriving every month in the United States, overwhelming state and local health departments.

Under its old immigration authority, the PHS went to work establishing an Office of Refugee Health and providing special supplemental grants to Community Health Centers in high impact areas. Commissioned officers from the PHS hospitals and elsewhere were mobilized on temporary assignments to screen and treat the new arrivals. Tuberculosis, hepatitis B, and mental illness were prevalent conditions for which special programs were developed under the direction of the CDC. The problem became more complicated in 1980, when Cuba suddenly reversed its ban on emigration and simultaneously discharged thousands of prisoners and mental patients resulting in the Mariel Boat Lift. At the same time, Haitians fleeing political oppression and poverty began arriving in large numbers, creating a public health crisis in South Florida. The Office of Refugee Health set up a triage center in Miami which, working with the Immigration and Naturalization Service, discharged the arrivals or sent them to one of four military camps in Florida, Arkansas, Pennsylvania, and Wisconsin which were staffed by commissioned personnel from the PHS hospitals. Although a few immigrants remained in long-term federal custody for criminal or psychiatric reasons, most were released to new lives in the United States. In all, some 900,000 Southeast Asians, 125,000 Cubans, and 15,000 Haitians were resettled without the outbreak of any major disease.

By the end of the 1970s, inflation and the federal budget deficit had become principal and inescapable political players not only on the national scene but in the arena of public health. Little by little, cost containment overshadowed concerns for equity in care in the policy debates that governed budgets, programs, and legislation. PHS appropriations—including that of NIH—barely kept pace with inflation. In discussions emblematic of the time, policymakers began to explore ways to close down the NHSC scholarship program and diffuse the large "inventory" of PHS-obligated health professionals that had been built up. Proprietary hospitals, prospective reimbursement, and "competition" in health care emerged as ideas on the ascent, and health planning, health manpower programs, and regulation came under increasing attack. In the meantime, events tangential to public health, including continued inflation, high interest rates, and the Iranian hostage crisis, were leading to the defeat of the sitting president and would, in time, move the new ideas from the realm of political theory to the reality of public health policy.

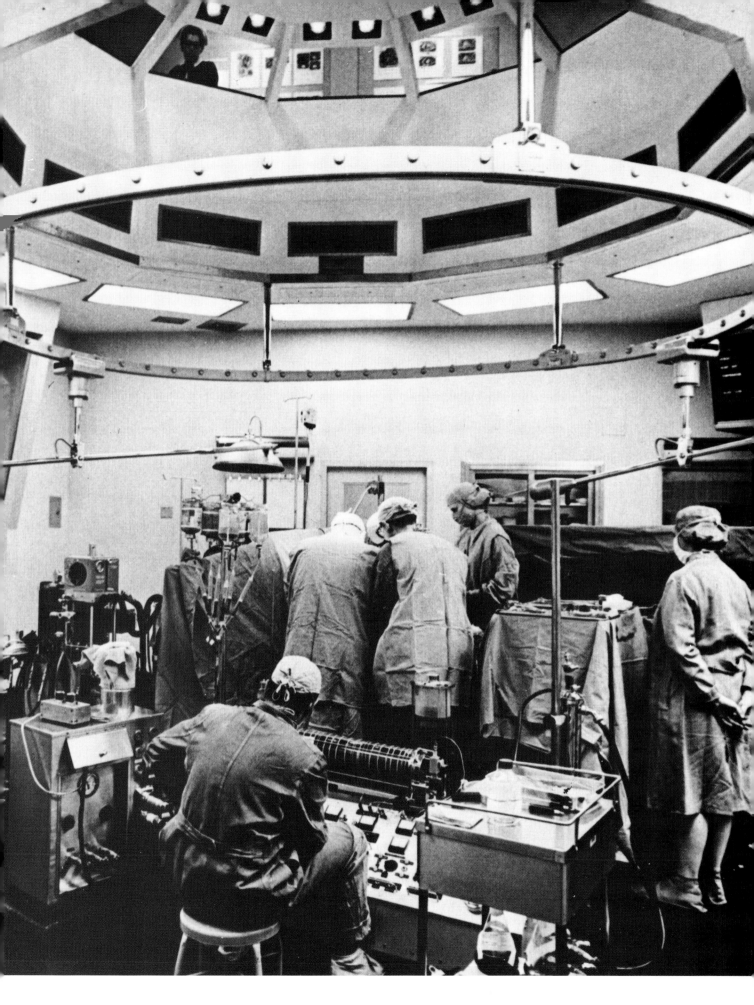

Chapter Nine
1981-1989

New Politics, New Plagues

We are fighting a disease—not people.

Surgeon General C. Everett Koop

Far from its genesis as the Marine Hospital Service, the PHS of the late 20th century is ubiquitous in American life. Issues such as AIDS, smoking, animal rights, product tampering, and genetic engineering, among others, are the domain of today's PHS. The regulation of radiation-emitting products, for example, such as suntanning devices (opposite) falls to the Food and Drug Administration.

In his inaugural address on January 20, 1981, President Ronald Reagan stated simply, "Government is not the solution to our problem. Government is the problem." With this proposition as philosophical compass, his new administration set about consolidating the domestic programs of the federal government and modifying them in keeping with the president's conservative principles. Deregulation, devolution (passing programs back to states), the disposal of "unnecessary" government assets, and pure budget cuts were the tools used by the Office of Management and Budget (OMB) in its stewardship of the Reagan policies. Strategists working at Washington-based institutions, such as the American Enterprise Institute and the Heritage Foundation, had done careful homework in the months prior to the Reagan election and were ready with specific administrative and legislative plans. In the health arena, those plans called for capping Medicaid, abolishing health planning, curtailing the National Health Service Corps and health manpower programs, converting many specific health programs into "block grants" to the states, and, once again, closing down the PHS hospitals.[1] The "Reagan Revolution" envisioned major changes in the PHS.

Reagan appointed Senate veteran, Richard Schweiker, as secretary of Health and Human Services. Schweiker made the decision to maintain the Surgeon Generalship but to separate it from the position of assistant secretary for health. For the latter post he chose Dr. Edward Brandt, the vice chancellor for health affairs of the University of Texas, a medical educator and a biostatistician with a record as a strong manager. For Surgeon General, Schweiker nominated fellow Pennsylvanian, Dr. C. Everett Koop, the surgeon-in-chief at Children's Hospital of Philadelphia and a distinguished pediatric surgeon whose work was internationally acclaimed.

Koop's appointment became the subject of immediate controversy inasmuch as he had no formal experience in public health and was an outspoken, pro-life activist. He came to Washington in March of 1981 in a temporary position as deputy to Brandt, awaiting Senate confirmation as the argument about his nomination grew. Liberal groups and public health organizations lined up to testify against him, criticizing his appointment as a "political gesture" to the right wing. For Koop, it was a terrible time, "the roughest time I have ever had in my life....There's no doubt about the fact that I became the lightning rod for an awful lot of things that the president himself was interested

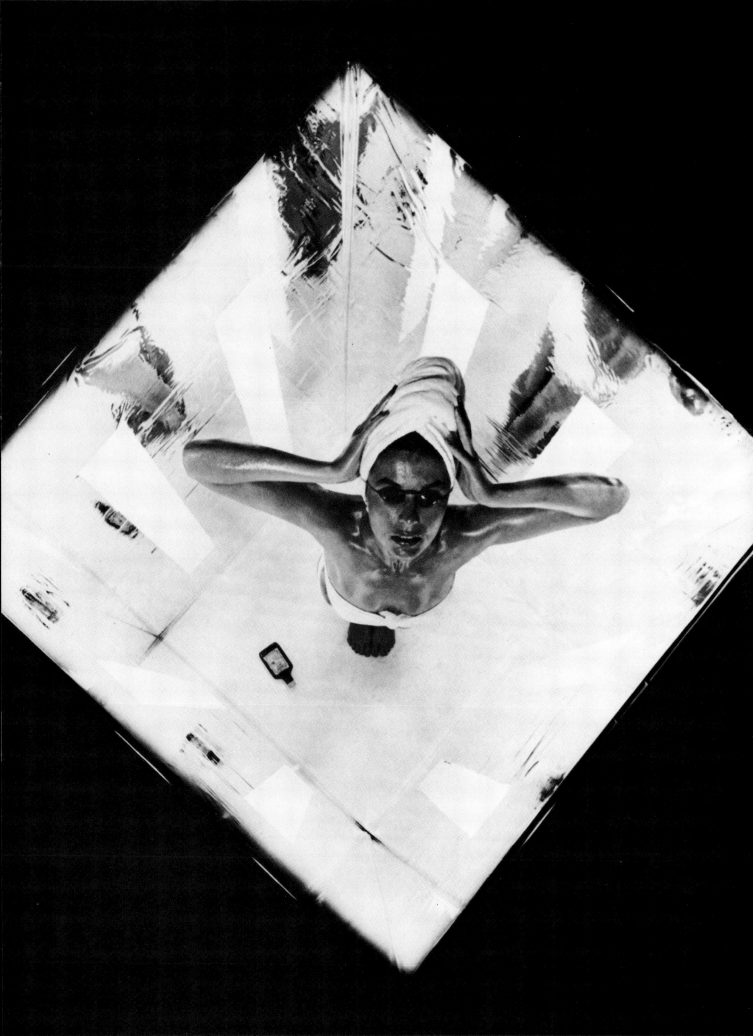

Usted es capaz
de dominar el español y inglés.

And you're still smoking?

Dr. C. Everett Koop (above) was appointed Surgeon General in 1981. He has devoted special attention to the continued antismoking campaign of the PHS (opposite), calling for a smoke-free society by the year 2000. His candor and common sense in dealing with AIDS, his outspokenness on behalf of the rights of the vulnerable, his program of revitalization for the Commissioned Corps, and his use of the uniform have given him and the office of Surgeon General great visibility. He has repeatedly stimulated the imaginations of America's political cartoonists (following pages).

"...IT HAS BEEN BROUGHT TO MY ATTENTION THAT WE MUST DEAL WITH A DEADLY DISEASE."

BASSET 4/29/87

THE LAST CIGARETTE SMOKER IN AMERICA

"HONEY... THE SURGEON GENERAL IS HERE TO SEE YOU..."

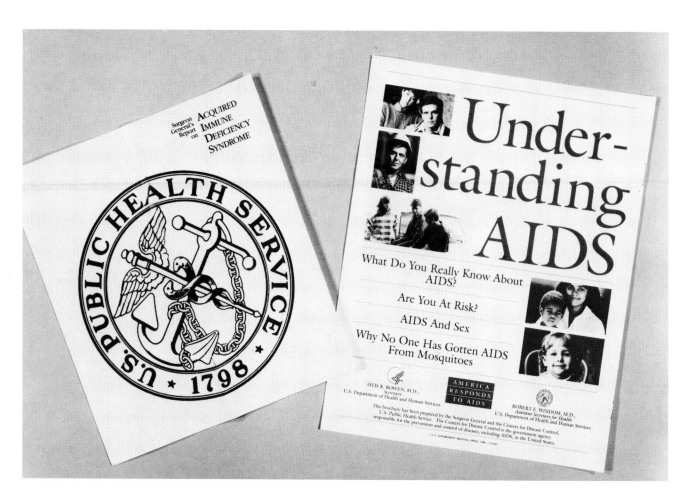

AIDS has been at the center of policy, program, and budget debates throughout the PHS since the syndrome was first observed early in the decade. Drs. Robert Gallo (opposite above) of the NIH and Luc Montagnier of the Institut Pasteur identified the viral agent of AIDS (opposite below) in 1984. Vice President George Bush (right) meets with the NIH AIDS executive committee in 1987 flanked by (left to right) Drs. James Wyngaarden, Anthony Fauci, and Vincent DeVita. The Surgeon General's AIDS report and the household mailing pamphlet (above) have been the centerpieces of the PHS public education campaign.

in, such as abortion."[2] Koop's ordeal ended on November 16, 1981 when, by a vote of sixty-eight to twenty-four, the Senate confirmed him as the thirteenth Surgeon General. His first appointment as Surgeon General was Dr. Faye Abdellah as Deputy Surgeon General—the first woman and the first nurse to hold the position.

The administration's strategy was to accomplish change through a single, massive bill rather than numerous smaller ones. That legislation was the Omnibus Budget Reconciliation Act (OBRA) of 1981 signed on August 13, a bare nine months after the Reagan election. Among the many elements of government it recast, OBRA collapsed a multiplicity of PHS programs into three block grants—alcohol, drug abuse, and mental health; preventive health services; and maternal and child health. Awarded on a formula basis, the block grants left wide discretion to the states in use of the money. The overall funding of the block grants constituted a budget cut of approximately 25 percent enacted on the premise—contested in many quarters—that the efficiency and flexibility of this system would offset the decreased support. OBRA included a primary care block grant that would have transferred the Community Health Center program to the states but its terms were so disadvantageous that, with two exceptions, the states chose to forgo it. While the block grants did not put the PHS out of business in these areas of public health, it did reverse a long-standing historical trend toward greater federal influence on state health programs.

OBRA also closed the PHS hospitals. Despite lobbying by maritime interests, Department of Defense beneficiaries, and representatives of the affected communities, OBRA terminated the health care entitlement for merchant seaman and required the immediate transfer or closure of the eight remaining hospitals and twenty-seven clinics. Five of the hospitals passed to community corporations, two to the Department of Defense, and one to the state of Louisiana. In New Orleans, a bitter-sweet jazz funeral featured pallbearers carrying a flag-draped casket and taps played by the city's Navy Band. The *Times Picayune* of October 4, 1981 reported that the hospital "...died Wednesday after a long fiscal illness....(It) was born in 1802 and had been a life long resident of New Orleans...."[3] Some hospital staff found employment with the successor institutions while others looked for PHS positions elsewhere resulting, ultimately, in major lay-offs throughout the system. The hospital closures also marked a milestone extraordinary in the life of any institution in that they made the PHS a historical orphan—an agency comprised entirely of programs added to its deceased, original mission. The continuity of the PHS, despite this loss, stands as evidence of its adaptability over time.

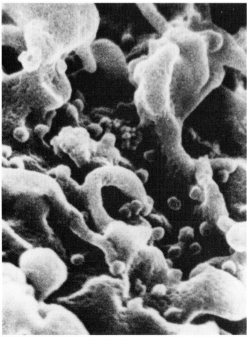

OBRA did not eliminate the family planning program or the migrant health program as the OMB had intended nor did it terminate health planning. It did curtail funding for the latter activity leading to

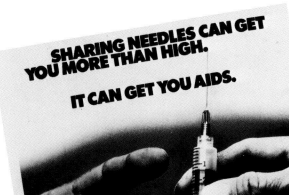

an eventual repeal of the law in 1986. The result of OBRA, however, was an effective budget cut for the PHS between 1980 and 1982 of more than 20 percent and a drop in the size of the Commissioned Corps from 7,300 in 1980 to 5,800 in 1983 and in the overall strength of the PHS from 56,000 to 48,000. Particularly hard-hit were the PHS agencies providing health care and health professional training, which led to the merger of the Health Services Administration with the Health Resources Administration to form the Health Resources and Services Administration (HRSA). In all, OBRA left the PHS a leaner organization.

The CDC's *Morbidity and Mortality Weekly Report* (MMWR) of June 5, 1981 ran a short article entitled "*Pneumocystis Pneumonia—Los Angeles*" which unwittingly announced the advent of a new epoch in human disease. "The occurrence of pneumocystosis in these five previously healthy individuals," editorialized MMWR, "without clinically apparent underlying immunodeficiency is unusual."[4] All of the early cases reported were homosexual men, leading to the assumption by many that this new syndrome was, in some way, caused by and limited to homosexuals. The men were, in fact, immunosuppressed and suffering from a new disease of global proportions—Acquired Immunodeficiency Syndrome (AIDS). The press and the public watched the CDC's struggle to understand the syndrome with increasing alarm as the lethal nature of the illness and its potential dimensions became apparent. In the summer of 1982, the first patient with hemophilia was diagnosed with AIDS, followed in the fall by a child who had been transfused, suggesting that the condition was passed by blood and blood products. Heterosexual and transplacental spread were subsequently identified, as was needle-borne transmission, threatening wide dissemination of AIDS among illicit drug users.

As the scope of the epidemic grew, so did fear. The PHS found itself at the center of controversy, with the gay community demanding more research and quicker results on one side, and conservative religious and political groups calling for quarantine on the other. "I didn't know what it was," recalls Brandt who was the man in the middle during this early period, "but I honestly believed at the time that it would turn out to be a tragic but simple problem. I was mistaken. It was not simple."[5] Brandt assembled and chaired a Public Health Service AIDS Task Force that regularly convened the principals from PHS agencies that were wrestling with the etiology and epidemiology of the disease. Lacking a cause, let alone a treatment, it was nonetheless clear to Brandt and his colleagues that AIDS was precipitated by a transmissible agent and that behavior modification and risk reduction programs were the only available interventions. In March of 1983, the

PHS published the first set of guidelines on AIDS prevention, recommending that high-risk individuals refrain from donating blood and modify their sexual practices. The problem became less mysterious in the spring of 1984 when Drs. Robert Gallo of the NIH and Luc Montagnier of the Institut Pasteur announced the identification of a new retrovirus as the agent of AIDS. This remarkable breakthrough led to the rapid development of an antibody test that could be used to screen donated blood as well as individuals for signs of the virus.

While the antibody test provided welcome protection for the blood supply, it resolved neither the prejudices nor the thorny ethical and practical issues that were swirling around AIDS. The president had been silent on the subject and many felt that there was an absence of political leadership in dealing with the epidemic. Certainly that was the perception of the Surgeon General who had been excluded from AIDS policy and strategy discussions prior to 1985. "In the first months of Reagan's second term," Koop recalled,

> I began to talk publicly about AIDS and before very long...I became the spokesman for AIDS; not because of any decision, but just by happenstance, the filling of a vacuum, the ability to articulate and, most of all, the refusal to politicize a health issue.[6]

The president then asked Koop to prepare a report on AIDS which, working for nine months, writing much of it himself, he did. Standing clearly on science and not on his own moral beliefs, the Surgeon General talked about sex education in grade schools and the use of condoms, denounced notions of quarantine, and called for tolerance. Released on October 22, 1986, the report was explicit, nonjudgmental, controversial, and popular. "Overnight I lost the constituencies I'd had," reflected Koop,

> which included right-wing conservatives, right-wing religious bodies, pro-life people and I gained all the liberals and moderates that weren't already with me. And I got the blessings of the people in public health.[7]

While the president never spoke publicly about the document, elements within the administration including domestic policy advisor Gary Bauer and Education Secretary William Bennett were furious and attacked the report and its premises.

Breaking on a society that believed contagious disease to be a scourge of the past, AIDS has tested public health leadership in the laboratory, in legislative bodies, and on the street. Dr. Samuel Broder of the National Cancer Institute developed AZT, an agent originally intended for cancer therapy, as the first drug effective in AIDS treatment and the FDA approved it for distribution in 1987. A significant decline in the rate of new infections among homosexuals suggested that public education worked well in some populations. Little change, however, has been recorded in the rate of transmission among drug addicts. In an effort to address the citizenry as a whole, the PHS sent

In the forty years since the establishment of the National Institute of Dental Research (NIDR), the dental health of Americans has improved markedly. The work of NIDR researcher Ann Davis (above) is assisted by computer imaging.

a copy of an eight-page brochure based on CDC guidelines but personally penned by the Surgeon General entitled "Understanding AIDS" to all 107 million households in the United States in the spring of 1988—the largest public health mailing ever done.

While taxing the resources of public health agencies at all levels, AIDS has also mobilized them. The epidemic has given a visibility and urgency to the work of the PHS that surely must have been familiar to leaders of earlier years who did regular battle with plague, yellow fever, and tuberculosis. Koop and Brandt have provided extraordinary leadership as have Drs. James Mason and James Curran who, respectively, headed the CDC and directed its AIDS efforts, Dr. Anthony Fauci who coordinated the NIH's AIDS activities, and Dr. Robert Windom who succeeded Brandt as assistant secretary for health. They have stepped forward as scientists and statesmen in this decade as Parran, Goldberger, and Stiles did in the past.

Koop, however, still had credibility problems with the Commissioned Corps. His high-profile positions on topics such as tobacco, organ transplantation, medical self-help, and the rights of the disabled, as well as AIDS, gave the Surgeon Generalship as much prominence as it had ever had. Yet the OMB and even HHS continued to question the relevance of the Commissioned Corps. In the winter of 1987, supported by HHS Secretary Otis Bowen and his chief of staff, Thomas Burke, Koop set about a revitalization of the Corps, assuming formal command authority over its 5,500 officers in April of that year, requiring the increased use of the uniform, invigorating the system of mobility in assignments, and promoting recruitment activities. He particularly sought to increase the number of women and minorities entering the Service. Koop appointed veteran PHS manager, Dr. Edward Martin, as his chief of staff to promote revitalization within the PHS and provide coordination with the Department of Defense and other federal agencies. "We'll make ninety percent of them (commissioned officers) extraordinarily happy—give them a new lease on life," Koop said of revitalization. "Ten percent will be furious. But that ten percent will be people who have subverted the system for their own agenda."[8] The results have confirmed the prediction and disarmed some of the Corps' most ardent critics. For the first time in four decades, the OMB spoke up in support of the Corps, a circumstance extolled by Koop on January 4, 1989, in a speech saluting the accomplishments of revitalization on the occasion of the Centennial of the Commissioned Corps.[9]

PHS vitality during the past decade has been evident in many areas. The CDC, whose name was pluralized in 1980 to the Centers for Disease Control, increased its emphasis on noninfectious illness, establishing a Center for Chronic Diseases and adding the Office of

Smoking and Health and the National Center for Health Statistics to its programs. In 1983, the responsibility for the health aspects of the Superfund Act was assumed by the PHS and established in tandem with the CDC as the Agency for Toxic Substances and Disease Registry. In 1988, under the leadership of its first Native American director, Dr. Everett Rhoades, the Indian Health Service was elevated to agency status within the PHS. This move reflected the IHS's maturation as an institution and the growth of support for Indian self-determination. The Health Resources and Services Administration survived the cutbacks early in the decade, maintaining a vigorous Community Health Center program and replacing the NHSC scholarships with a state-federal loan repayment program for physicians working in underserved areas.

In the spirit of deregulation and under the gun of AIDS, Frank Young, commissioner of the FDA, has labored to expedite and improve the approval process for new drugs. The agency has continued to develop its role in the regulation of medical devices while responding to periodic product-tampering crises and sorting out the potential health hazards posed by chemicals in the food chain. With block grants transferring much of the responsibility for behavioral health services to the states, ADAMHA has emphasized research in the neurosciences, believing that new knowledge is needed to produce solu-

Two out of every five FDA employees in 1989 are scientists. FDA molecular biologists Douglas Archer and Keith Lampel (opposite), use computer-generated graphics in their investigation into the virulence of bacteria isolated from food. Two workers from the Agency for Toxic Substances and Disease Registry (ATSDR) in full protective gear (above) prepare for an investigation. The ATSDR was created by Congress and placed in the PHS to implement the health-related aspects of the "Superfund" law, which mandates the cleanup of hazardous waste sites.

The old and the new, the traditional and
the contemporary, the spiritual and the
scientific, meet in the Indian Health
Service. A family arrives at the Sells,
Arizona IHS hospital.

tions to the treatment and prevention of mental and addictive disorders. Today, ADAMHA supports 85 percent of the nation's biomedical and behavioral research on alcohol, drug abuse, and mental illness. Nonetheless, many of the country's most topical public health issues—drug addiction, AIDS, homelessness, and the care of the chronically mentally ill—are in the domain of ADAMHA. In response, the agency has created an Office of Substance Abuse Prevention, dramatically increased the proportion of its budget devoted to AIDS, and has continued its support of the family movement in the mental health area.

With a 1989 budget of $6.5 billion dollars, the NIH accounts for almost one-half of the PHS appropriation. Basic research that explores the cell on a molecular and submolecular level has flourished. Yet the very success of this work as well as demands of global economic competition have tended to narrow and blur old distinctions between basic and applied research. The therapeutic products of genetic engineering such as hepatitis B vaccine and insulin, or new diagnostic tools such as magnetic resonance imaging have moved rapidly from the laboratory to the market place. Although commercialization of the results of NIH-sponsored, basic research by private industry has created controversy over what degree of private gain might stem from public patronage, it has also greatly accelerated the pace at which new biomedical knowledge is translated into use. The speed with which AZT was identified, tested, and marketed is testimony to the cooperation of government and industry as well as the collaboration of the laboratory at the front line of public health practice.

And yet, many health problems remain beyond the grasp of the PHS. Thirty-seven million Americans have no health insurance, more than a million people are infected with the AIDS virus, almost one-third of adults still smoke, the nation is in the grip of an epidemic of illicit drug use, the homicide rate in the United States is among the highest in the world, and the infant mortality rate remains worse than that of fifteen other nations. All of these circumstances have complex social and political roots with ill health being but a common element. The PHS now, as in the past, can count and articulate these problems far more easily than it can solve them. But so it was with tuberculosis and pellagra. The PHS tracked venereal disease and engaged in venereal disease health education campaigns long before effective treatment was possible. Technical achievements eventually defeated polio, political determination revolutionized the health of Indians, and technical *and* political commitment eradicated smallpox.

As in the past, the tonics for today's public health dilemmas will certainly come from a blend of science and government. Just as certainly, the PHS will be a part of those solutions, mediating as it always has, between the laboratory and the law, the individual and the government, the plagues and the politics.

Notes

Chapter One

1. Ralph C. Williams, *The United States Public Health Service, 1798-1950* (Washington, D.C.: The Commissioned Officers Association of the United States Public Health Service, [1951]), p.26.

2. *Ibid.*, p. 27.

3. An Act for the relief of sick and disabled seamen. July 16, 1798 (I Stat. L., 605-606).

4. An excellent discussion of the first seventy years of the Marine Hospital Fund as well as the subsequent reforms is provided by Robert Straus, *Medical Care for Seamen: The Origin of Public Medical Service in the United States* (New Haven: Yale University Press, 1950) in his chapters entitled "The Unorganized Marine Hospital Fund" and "The Reorganized Marine Hospital Service," pp. 32-88.

5. Letter from Evan Jones to the Secretary of State, dated August 10, 1801, Commerce and Navigation, I, 493, *American State Papers*, VII as quoted by Straus, p. 36.

6. Richard H. Thurm, *For the Relief of the Sick and Disabled: The U.S. Public Health Service Hospital at Boston, 1799-1969* (Washington, D.C.: GPO, 1972) (#1729-0010), pp. 41-58. For another useful account of the Boston hospital see John W. Trask, *The United States Marine Hospital, Port of Boston: An Account of Its Origin and Briefly of Its History and of the Physicians Who Have Been in Charge* ([Washington, D.C.]: Federal Security Agency, U.S. Public Health Service, 1940).

7. Charles H. Stedman, "Report of Cases in the U.S. Marine Hospital, Chelsea," *The Boston Medical and Surgical Journal* 15, no. 16 (November 23, 1936): 245-251.

8. O. H. Brownson, Letter to George Bancroft dated December 22, 1840, cited by Thurm, p. 325.

9. G. B. Loring and T. B. Edwards, "Report upon the Subject of Marine Hospitals," as quoted by Williams, p. 45.

10. William M. Gouge, "Report on Marine Hospitals," *Senate Executive Documents*, 34th Cong., 1st sess., 1855, Vol. 5, no. 53, pp. 246-247.

11. George S. Boutwell summarizing Billings report on the Marine Hospitals in the 1869 *Annual Report* of the U. S. Treasury Department, quoted by Bess Furman, *A Profile of the United States Public Health Service, 1798-1948* (Washington, D.C.:

U.S. Department of Health, Education, and Welfare, 1973) (DHEW Pub. No. (NIH) 73-369), p. 115.

12. U.S. Marine Hospital Service, *Annual Report*, 1875, (Washington, D.C.), p. 6.

13. For a good, short summary of the National Board of Health see Wilson G. Smillie, "The National Board of Health 1879-1883," in *Public Health: Its Promise for the Future* (New York: Macmillan, 1955), pp. 331-339. Furman treats the subject in an interesting but intermittent and anecdotal fashion on pp. 139-189. Also extant is an unpublished manuscript by Wyndham Miles, *The History of the National Board of Health, 1879-1893*, National Library of Medicine, History of Medicine Division.

14. Figures taken from U.S. Marine Hospital Service *Annual Report*.

15. Walter Wyman, "River Exposure and Its Effects upon the Lung," U. S. Marine Hospital Service, *Annual Report*, 1877, p. 164.

16. Figures taken from the U.S. Marine Hospital Service *Annual Report*.

17. U. S. Marine Hospital Service, *Annual Report*, 1885, p.10.

18. *Ibid.*, p. 11.

Chapter Two

1. Personnel and budget figures on the U. S. Marine Hospital/Public Health Service have been developed from the *Annual Report* and from documents supplied by the Office of Management of the Office of the Assistant Secretary for Health of the Department of Health and Human Services. Deposited in the Commissioned Corps Centennial Archive at the History of Medicine Division, National Library of Medicine, Bethesda, Maryland.

2. Cited by Furman, p. 203

3. U.S. Congress, House Committee on Ventilation and Acoustics, *Ventilation of the House of Representatives*, 53rd Cong., 2nd sess., May 8, 1894, H. Rpt. 853, cited by Furman, p. 213.

4. See Victoria Harden, *Inventing the NIH: Federal Biomedical Research Policy, 1887-1937* (hereinafter, *Inventing the NIH*) (Baltimore: Johns Hopkins University Press, 1986), for an excellent discussion of the early years of the Hygienic Laboratory and its role in the U.S. Marine Hospital/Public Health Service.

5. Quoted from Dr. W. H. Kellogg of

the San Francisco Board of Health and cited by Furman, p. 244.

6. Samuel B. Grubbs, *By Order of the Surgeon General: Thirty-seven Years Active Duty in the Public Health Service* (Greenfield, Indiana: Wm. Mitchell Printing Co., 1943), p.72.

7. Terence V. Powderly, "The Immigrant Menace to National Health," *American Review*, 175 (July 1902): 53-60, as cited by Alan M. Kraut, "Silent Travelers: Germs, Genes, and American Efficiency, 1890-1924," *Social Science History*, 12, no. 4(Winter 1988): 377.

8. E. H. Mullan, "Mental Examination of Immigrants: Administration and Line Inspection at Ellis Island," *Public Health Reports*, May 18, 1917, pp.733-746.

9. Victor Heiser, *An American Doctor's Odyssey: Adventures in Forty-five Countries* (New York: W. W. Norton, 1936), pp. 14-15.

10. See Kraut.

11. U. S. Public Health and Marine Hospital Service, *Annual Report*, 1902.

12. Leslie Lumsden quoted by Furman, p.291

13. Milton Rosenau as quoted by Wilson G. Smillie, *Public Health: Its Promise for the Future* (New York: Macmillan, 1955), p. 468.

Chapter Three

1. Franklin MacVeagh, U.S. Department of the Treasury, *Annual Report*, cited by Furman, p. 281.

2. Rupert Blue as quoted by Furman, p. 305.

3. Henry Rose Carter manuscript entitled "Note on the Spread of Yellow Fever in Houses—Extrinsic Incubation," reproduced by Williams, p. 260.

4. Letter from Walter Reed to Henry Rose Carter dated February 26, 1901, as quoted by Furman, p. 241.

5. See John Ettling, *The Germ of Laziness: Rockefeller Philanthropy and Public Health in the New South* (Cambridge: Harvard University Press, 1981) for a thorough account of the work of Stiles.

6. Victoria Harden, personal communication.

7. John McMullen as quoted by Furman, p. 289.

8. Joseph Goldberger as quoted by Furman, p. 302.

9. See Elizabeth W. Etheridge, *The Butterfly Caste: A Social History of Pellagra in the South* (Westport, Connecticut:

Greenwood Press, 1972) for a full discussion of Goldberger's work in the context of southern social history.

10. Leslie Lumsden, letter submitted to the Surgeon General on November 16, 1917, as quoted by Williams, p. 569.

11. Grubbs, pp. 298-299.

12. *Ibid.*, p. 292.

13. Alice C. Evans, *Memoirs*, p. 33, an unpublished manuscript on file at the History of Medicine Division, National Library of Medicine, Bethesda, Maryland.

14. Laurence F. Schmeckebier, *The Public Health Service: Its History, Activities and Organization* (Baltimore: Johns Hopkins Press, 1923), pp. 56-75 provides a detailed, factual discussion of the relationship between the PHS, the War Risk Insurance Board, and the Veterans' Bureau.

15. U.S. Public Health Service, *Annual Report*, 1920, p.236.

16. Figures provided by the Division of Commissioned Personnel, United States Public Health Service, Rockville, Maryland. PHS personnel data provided by this and other sources is deposited in the Commissioned Corps Centennial Archive, History of Medicine Division, National Library of Medicine, Bethesda,Maryland.

Chapter Four

1. "Hugh Cumming," *New York Times Magazine*, June 10, 1928, p. 17, as quoted by Harden, *Inventing the NIH*, p. 53.

2. E. H. Mullan, "Mental Deficiency: Some of its Public Health Aspects, with Reference to Diagnosis," *Public Health Reports*, Reprint No. 236 (November 27, 1914): 2.

3. Leroy Burney, interviewed by Fitzhugh Mullan, October 17, 1988. The interview is deposited in the Commissioned Corps Centennial Archive at the History of Medicine Division, National Library of Medicine, Bethesda, Maryland.

4. See James H. Jones, *Bad Blood: The Tuskegee Syphilis Experiment* (hereinafter, *Bad Blood*) (New York: Free Press, c1981) for a full discussion of the Tuskegee Syphilis Project and the PHS VD program in the South.

5. James A. Tobey, *The National Government and Public Health* (Baltimore: Johns Hopkins Press, 1926), pp. 380-386.

6. "Chemistry and Disease," *New York Times*, July 7, 1926, p. 24, as quoted by Harden, *Inventing the NIH*, p. 104.

7. W. Palmer Dearing, interviewed by

Fitzhugh Mullan, October 21, 1988. The interview is deposited in the Commissioned Corps Centennial Archive at the History of Medicine Division, National Library of Medicine, Bethesda, Maryland.

8. Joseph Mountin as quoted by Alexander Langmuir in Elizabeth Etheridge's unpublished manuscript, *The Believers: A History of the CDC* (hereinafter, *The Believers*), p. 362.

9. Joseph Mountin, from an address given to the 48th Annual Session of the Ohio Welfare Conference, Columbus, Ohio, October 4-7, 1938, as reprinted in *Selected Papers of Joseph W. Mountin, M.D.* (n.p.: Joseph W. Mountin Memorial Committee, 1956), p. 4.

10. Burney/Mullan interview.

11. Susan Volkmar, "The Public Health Service—From the Distaff Side," *Commissioned Corps Bulletin* 3, no. 4 (April 1989): 2.

12. Cited by George Rosen, *A History of Public Health* (New York: MD Publications, c1958), p. 459.

Chapter Five

1. Thomas Parran, "Health Services of Tomorrow," *Public Health Reports* 49, no. 15 (April 13, 1934): 479.

2. *Saturday Evening Post*, December 12, 1938, as quoted by Furman, p. 404.

3. "A National Health Program: Report of the Technical Committee on Medical Care," as quoted by Paul Starr, *The Social Transformation of American Medicine* (New York: Basic Books, 1982), p. 276.

4. Burney/Mullan interview.

5. Dearing/Mullan interview.

6. The history of the Federal Security Agency is discussed by Rufus Miles, *The Department of Health, Education, and Welfare* (New York: Praeger, [c1974]), pp. 17-24.

7. This account of the work of Trendley Dean and the dental research group is drawn from Ruth Ray Harris, *Dental Services in a New Age: A History of the National Institute of Dental Research* (Rockville, Maryland: Montrose Press, 1989) and a booklet published by the National Institute of Dental Research and the National Library of Medicine on the occasion of the 40th anniversary of the NIDR entitled *American Contributions to the New Age of Dental Research* ([Bethesda, Maryland?]: U.S. Department of Health and Human Services, Public

Health Service, National Institutes of Health, National Institute of Dental Research, National Library of Medicine, 1988).

8. As quoted by W. Palmer Dearing.

9. Records of the United States Coast Guard Cutter *Comanche* as quoted by Williams, p. 668.

10. Ralph R. Braund as quoted by Williams, p. 675.

11. Coast Guard records as quoted by Williams, p. 683.

12. Victoria A. Harden, *Rocky Mountain Spotted Fever: A Twentieth Century Disease* (Baltimore: Johns Hopkins University Press, forthcoming), Chap. 9.

13. Margaret Pittman, "The Regulation of Biologic Products, 1902-1972," in Harriet R. Greenwald and Victoria A. Harden, eds., *Intramural Contributions, 1887-1977* (Bethesda, Maryland: National Institute of Allergy and Infectious Diseases, 1987), pp. 61-70.

14. See Daniel M. Fox, "The Politics of the NIH Extramural Program, 1937-1950," *The Journal of the History of Medicine and Allied Sciences* 42(1987): 447-466.

15. The history of the Cadet Nurse Corps is detailed well in Federal Security Agency, Public Health Service, *The Cadet Nurse Corps and Other Federal Nurse Training Programs* (Washington, D.C.: GPO, 1950) (PHS Pub. No. 38) from which this account is drawn.

16. John C. Eason, Jr., interviewed by Fitzhugh Mullan, October 26, 1988. The interview is deposited in the Commissioned Corps Centennial Archive at the History of Medicine Division, National Library of Medicine, Bethesda, Maryland.

17. Etheridge, *The Believers*, gives a good account of Mountin's influence in the founding of the CDC in chapters 1 and 2.

18. U.S. Public Health Service, *Facts about the Hill-Burton Program, July 1, 1947-June 30, 1971* (Rockville, Maryland, [1971]), as quoted by Starr, p. 350.

Chapter Six

1. *NIH Almanac* (Bethesda, Maryland: U.S. Department of Health, Education, and Welfare, Public Health Service, National Institutes of Health, 1983),(DHHS, NIH Pub. No. 83-5, March, 1983), p. 121, 133.

2. Leonard Scheele, *New York Times Oral History Program: Columbia University Oral History Collection*, Part III, No. 93, October 16, 1967, pp. 31-32.

3. *Ibid.*, p. 34.

4. For comments on the McCarthy period in the PHS see Scheele's Columbia interview, p. 26-28; Dearing's interview; Furman's unpublished manuscript, Chap. 20, pp. 26-27a; and Etheridge, *The Believers*, p. 118.

5. This discussion of HEW draws on Rufus Miles, *The Department of Health, Education, and Welfare* (New York: Praeger, 1974), pp. 25-33.

6. This discussion is derived from Furman, unpublished manuscript, Chap. 20, pp. 1-22; and Edward Shorter, *The Health Century* (New York: Doubleday, 1987), pp. 60-70.

7. Scheele's Columbia interview, p. 7.

8. Ray Shaw, interviewed by John Todd, March 19, 1985, Tucson, Arizona, p. 7. The interview is deposited in the Commissioned Corps Centennial Archive at the History of Medicine Division, National Library of Medicine, Bethesda, Maryland.

9. Shaw/Todd interview, p. 11. No full history of the Indian Health Service exists currently. Other documents on the early history of health services to Indians and the formation of the Indian Health Service include Ruth M. Raup, *The Indian Health Program from 1800-1955* (Washington, D.C.: Public Health Service, 1959); *Indian Health Service Chart Series Book* (Public Health Service, Indian Health Service, April, 1988); and multiple historical summaries prepared by John Todd, a retired Indian Health Service officer. These documents are deposited in the Commissioned Corps Centennial Archive at the History of Medicine Division, National Library of Medicine, Bethesda, Maryland.

10. William Stewart, interviewed by Fitzhugh Mullan, September 28, 1988. The interview is deposited in the Commissioned Corps Centennial Archive at the History of Medicine Division, National Library of Medicine, Bethesda, Maryland.

11. Alexander Langmuir, "The Epidemic Intelligence Service of the Center for Disease Control," *Public Health Reports* 95, no. 5 (September-October, 1980): 473.

12. Burney/Mullan interview.

13. Leonard Dworsky, personal communication; and Leonard Dworsky, *Conservation in the United States: A Documentary History* (New York: Chelsea House, 1971), pp. 276-284, 313-318, 320-335.

14. Leroy Burney, *Report on Environmental Health Problems*, Hearings before the Subcommittee of the Committee on Appropriations, 85th Cong., 2nd sess., as quoted by Furman, unpublished manuscript, Chap. 21, p. 32.

15. Leroy Burney, interviewed by Bess Furman, January 25, 1966, as quoted in Furman, unpublished manuscript, Chap. 21, p. 6.

16. U.S. Public Health Service, Study Group on Mission and Organization of the Public Health Service, *Final Report* (Washington, D.C.: GPO, 1960) (0—553903), p. 7.

Chapter Seven

1. Stewart/Mullan interview.

2. Leroy Burney, "Smoking and Lung Cancer: A Statement of the Public Health Service," *Journal of the American Medical Association* 171(1959): 1829-1837.

3. U.S. Surgeon General's Advisory Committee on Smoking and Health, *Smoking and Health: Report of the Advisory Committee to the Surgeon General of the Public Health Service* (Washington, D. C.: GPO, [1964]) (PHS Pub. No. 1103).

4. Stewart/Mullan interview.

5. A complete review of the smoking and health story can be found in: U.S. Department of Health and Human Services, *Reducing the Health Consequences of Smoking: 25 Years of Progress. A Report of the Surgeon General* (U.S. Department of Health and Human Services, Public Health Service, Centers for Disease Control, Center for Chronic Disease Prevention and Health Promotion, Office on Smoking and Health) (DHHS Pub. No. (CDC) 89-8411), prepublication version, January 11, 1989.

6. U.S. Department of Health and Human Services, Bureau of Health Professions, *Supply of Manpower in Selected Health Occupations: 1950-1990* ([Hyattsville, Maryland?]: U.S. Department of Health and Human Services, Health Resources Administration, Bureau of Health Professions, Division of Health Professions Analysis, 1980) (HRA No. 80-35), pp. 10, 16.

7. Philip Lee, interviewed by Fitzhugh Mullan, October 8, 1988. The interview is deposited in the Commissioned Corps Centennial Archive at the History of Medicine Division, National Library of Medicine, Bethesda, Maryland.

8. Alice Sardell, *The U.S. Experiment in Social Medicine: The Community Health Center Program, 1965-1986* (Pittsburgh, Pennsylvania: The University of Pittsburgh Press, 1988), pp. 50-53; and H. Jack Geiger, "Community Health Centers: Health Care as an Instrument of Social Change," in Victor Sidel and Ruth Sidel, eds., *Reforming Medicine: Lessons of the Last Quarter Century* (New York: Pantheon Books, c1984), pp. 11-14.

9. Personal communication from John H. Kelso.

10. John Gardner, *Public Health Service World*, December 1965, p. 2.

11. Rufus R. Miles, Jr., *The Department of Health, Education, and Welfare* (New York: Praeger, 1974), p. 193.

12. Lee/Mullan interview.

13. David Sencer, Centers for Disease Control oral history, April 19, 1983 as quoted by Etheridge, *The Believers*, p. 329.

14. Stewart/Mullan interview.

15. Lee/Mullan interview.

16. See Horace G. Ogden, *CDC and the Smallpox Crusade* (Washington, D.C.: U.S. Department of Health and Human Services, Public Health Service, Centers for Disease Control, 1987) (DHHS, Pub. No. (CDC) 87-8400), for a good summary discussion of the Global Smallpox Eradication Program and the CDC's role in it.

Chapter Eight

1. U.S. Department of Health, Education, and Welfare. Secretary's Committee to Study the Public Health Service Commissioned Corps. *Report* (Washington, D.C.: U.S. Department of Health, Education, and Welfare, [1971]), pp. 11, 57, 58.

2. *Washington Report on Health and Medicine* 1252(June 28, 1971): 2.

3. Jesse Steinfeld, *Memo*, To Members of the Commissioned Corps, June 24, 1971.

4. Merlin K. DuVal, interviewed by Fitzhugh Mullan, December 15, 1988. The interview is deposited in the Commissioned Corps Centennial Archive at the History of Medicine Division, National Library of Medicine, Bethesda, Maryland.

5. This discussion draws on Williams as well as Henry N. Doyle, *The Federal Industrial Hygiene Agency: A History of the Division of Occupational Health, United States Public Health Service*, prepared for the History of Industrial Hygiene Committee, American Conference of Governmen-

tal Hygienists, unpublished manuscript (1972?) provided by Mrs. Henry Doyle and deposited in the Commissioned Corps Centennial Archive at the History of Medicine Division, National Library of Medicine, Bethesda, Maryland. The 1987 Lucas Lecture of the Royal College of Physicians by J. Donald Millar, "Attempts at Strategic Thinking in Occupational Public Health" and an interview with Dr. Millar were also contributory.

6. The chronology and nature of PHS reorganization has been summarized in a very useful fashion in: U.S. Public Health Service, Office of the Assistant Secretary for Health, Office of Organization and Management Systems, *Historical Profile of the Leadership of the Public Health Service, 1944-1988* ([Rockville, Maryland?]: The Service, 1988).

7. Theodore Cooper, interviewed by Fitzhugh Mullan on October 13, 1988. The interview is deposited in the Commissioned Corps Centennial Archive at the History of Medicine Division, National Library of Medicine, Bethesda, Maryland.

8. James H. Jones, *Bad Blood*, provides a thorough treatment of the Tuskeegee Project.

9. Arthur M. Silverstein, *Pure Politics and Impure Science: The Swine Flu Affair* (Baltimore: Johns Hopkins University Press, 1981); and Richard E. Neustadt and Harvey V. Fineberg, *The Epidemic That Never Was: Policy Making and the Swine Flu Affair* (New York: Vintage Books, 1983) provide good documentation and significantly different interpretations of the swine flu experience.

10. A good discussion of the Community Health Center program is provided by Alice Sardell, *The U.S. Experiment in Social Medicine: The Community Health Center Program, 1965-1986* (Pittsburgh, Pennsylvania: University of Pittsburgh Press, 1988). An insightful essay on the development of the health center movement is found in H. Jack Geiger, "Community Health Centers: Health Care as an Instrument of Social Change" in Sidel and Sidel, eds., pp. 11-32.

11. Laurence J. Platt, "Proposal to Develop Legislation Enabling the Establishment of a National Health Corps in the U.S. Public Health Service," manuscript dated September 12, 1969. The fascinating and unlikely story of the enactment of the National Health Service Corps legislation is told in Eric Redman, *The Dance of Legislation* (New York:

Simon and Schuster, c1973). See Fitzhugh Mullan, "The National Health Service Corps and Health Personnel Innovations: Beyond Poorhouse Medicine," in Sidel and Sidel, eds., pp. 176-200, for further discussion and analysis of the National Health Service Corps.

12. Joseph Califano, Jr., "The Secretary's Foreword," in: U.S. Office of the Assistant Secretary for Health and Surgeon General, *Healthy People: The Surgeon General's Report on Health Promotion and Disease Prevention* (Washington, D.C.: GPO, 1979) (DHEW (PHS) Pub. No. 79-55071), p. viii.

13. Julius B. Richmond, interviewed by Fitzhugh Mullan, December 5, 1988. The interview is deposited in the Commissioned Corps Centennial Archive at the History of Medicine Division, National Library of Medicine, Bethesda, Maryland.

Chapter Nine

1. See Charles L. Heatherly, ed., *Mandate for Leadership: Policy Management in a Conservative Administration* (Washington, D.C.: Heritage Foundation, c1981), pp. 270-291 for an analytic discussion of the PHS.

2. C. Everett Koop, interviewed by Fitzhugh Mullan, February 6, 1989. The interview is deposited in the Commissioned Corps Centennial Archive at the History of Medicine Division, National Library of Medicine, Bethesda, Maryland.

3. New Orleans *Times Picayune*, October 4, 1981, p. 1.

4. "Pneumocystis Pneumonia—Los Angeles," *MMWR* 39(June 5, 1981): 250-251.

5. Edward N. Brandt, interviewed by Fitzhugh Mullan on December 20, 1988. The interview is deposited in the Commissioned Corps Centennial Archive at the History of Medicine Division, National Library of Medicine, Bethesda, Maryland.

6. Koop/Mullan interview.

7. Koop/Mullan interview.

8. Koop/Mullan interview.

9. C. Everett Koop, "Remarks Presented at the 100th Anniversary of the P.H.S. Commissioned Corps," January 4, 1989, unpublished, p. 15. The text of this address is deposited in the Commissioned Corps Centennial Archive at the History of Medicine Division, National Library of Medicine, Bethesda, Maryland.

Illustration
Credits

Abbreviations used in credits:

ADAMHA—Alcohol, Drug Abuse and
  Mental Health Administration.
ATSDR—Agency for Toxic Substances
  and Disease Registry.
CDC—Centers for Disease Control.
FDA—Food and Drug Administration.
FSA—Farm Security Administration.
NA—National Archives.
NCI—National Cancer Institute.
NGS—National Geographic Society.
NHLBI—National Heart, Lung, and
  Blood Institute.
NIAAA—National Institute on Alcohol
  Abuse and Alcoholism.
NIDR—National Institute of Dental
  Research.
NIH—National Institutes of Health.
NINCDS—National Institute of Neurolog-
  ical and Communicative Disorders and
  Stroke.
NIOSH—National Institute for Occupa-
  tional Safety and Health.
NLM—National Library of Medicine.
OSH/CDC—Office on Smoking and
  Health, Center for Chronic Disease
  Prevention and Health Promotion,
  Centers for Disease Control.
PD/NIH—Pharmacy Department, War-
  ren Grant Magnuson Clinical Center,
  National Institutes of Health.
PHS—Public Health Service.
SEHM—Saint Elizabeths Hospital
  Museum.
SI—Division of Medical Sciences,
  National Museum of American History,
  Smithsonian Institution.
VIC/NIH—Visitor Information Center,
  National Institutes of Health.

Chapter One
Page 15 SI; 16 above NLM, below NLM;
18 below left SI, below right NLM; 18 &
19 NLM; 20 above SI, below NLM; 21
NLM; 22 NLM; 23 NLM; 24 & 25 NLM;
25 NLM; 26 NLM; 27 above *Harper's
Weekly* 2:581, 1858/NLM, below *Harper's
Weekly* 1:324, 1857/NLM; 28 & 29 above
NA photo no. 90-G-1-1; 28 below NLM;
30 & 31 below CDC; 31 above NLM.

Chapter Two
Page 33 NLM; 34 NLM; 35 NA; 36 above
SI, below NLM; 36 & 37 NLM; 37 NLM;
38 NLM; 39 NLM; 40 NA; 41 above
NLM, below NLM; 42 NLM; 43 NLM; 44
above NLM, below NLM; 46 NLM; 47
NA photo no. 90-G-146-152; 48 NLM; 49
above NLM, below NLM; 50 above NA
photo no. 90-G-169-312, below NLM; 51
above NLM, below NA photo no.
90-G-58-6; 52 above NLM, below Courtesy of Hugh Mullan; 53 From: Grubbs,
Samuel B., *By Order of the Surgeon General.* Greenfield, Indiana : Press of Wm.
Mitchell, 1942.; 54 above NA photo no.
90-G-184-6, below NA photo no.
90-G-185-4; 55 above NA photo no.
90-G-184-8, below NA photo no.
90-G-184-5; 57 above NLM, below left
NLM, below right NA photo no.
90-G-184-7.

Chapter Three
Page 59 NA photo no. 90-G-42-1; 60
above NA photo no. 90-G-53-4, below
NLM; 61 NGS; 62 above NA photo no.
90-G-44-2885; 62 & 63 NA photo no.
90-G-44-2514; 63 NA; 64 above NLM,
below left FSA/Ben Shahn, photographer,
below right PHS; 65 NA photo no.
90-G-17-1; 66 & 67 PHS; 67 PHS; 68 NA
photo no. 90-G-38-3; 68 & 69 NA photo
no. 90-G-37-3; 70 NA photo no. 90-G-37-2;
71 NLM; 73 above left NLM, above right
NA photo no. 90-G-39-22, below NA
photo no. 90-G-41-2; 74 NA photo no.
90-G-28-2; 75 above NLM, below NA; 76
above NLM, below NGS; 76 & 77 PHS;
77 below NGS; 78 & 79 Iowa State University Library; 79 NLM; 80 SI; 80 & 81
NA photo no. 90-G-47-654.

Chapter Four
Page 83 PHS; 84 above PHS, below left
NA photo no. 90-G-49-20, below right
NA photo no. 90-G-49-17; 87 above left
NLM, above right NA 90-G-200-175,
below NA photo no. 90-G-200-177; 88 NA
photo no. 90-G-132-PHSB3036; 89 above
NA photo no. 90-G-128-2492, below-
NLM; 91 above NA photo no. 90-G-5-8,
below left NLM, below right NA photo
no. 90-G-5-7; 92 above NA photo no.
90-G-109-DN151; 92 & 93 PHS; 93 above
left NA photo no. 90-G-95-7A, above
right PHS; 94 PHS; 95 PHS; 96 PHS; 97
PHS; 98 & 99 PHS/Russell Lee, photographer; 98 below PHS/Russell Lee, photographer; 100 above NLM, below Courtesy
of Leroy Burney; 101 PHS; 103 above left
PHS/Marthey, photographer, above right
PHS, below NLM.

Chapter Five
Page 105 NLM; 106 & 107 NLM; 108 &
109 Drawing by Boris Artzybasheff in *Fortune*, May 6, 1941, pp. 80-18, reprinted by
permission; 190 NLM; 110 above left
NLM, below left PHS, below right PHS/
Arthur Rothstein, photographer; 111
PHS; 112 NLM; 113 above NLM, below
NLM; 114 NLM; 115 Courtesy of Mike
Randolph, FDA; 117 above left NLM,
above right NLM, below NLM; 118 PHS;
119 above U.S. Coast Guard Official
Photo/PHS, below U.S. Coast Guard Official Photo/PHS; 120 & 121 CDC; 121
right CDC; 122 & 123 CDC; 124 above
NLM, below left PHS, below right PHS;
126 NIDR; 127 above left PHS, above
right NLM, below NIDR.

Chapter Six
Page 129 PHS; 130 above PHS, below
PHS; 131 PHS; 132 & 133 PHS; 134 NLM;
135 Courtesy of Allen Brands; 136 NLM;
137 above NLM, below left NLM, below
right NLM; 138 above Courtesy of Fred
Rueter, below PD/NIH; 139 PHS; 140
above NA photo no. 306-PS-437-49-7698,
below NA photo no. 306-PS-437-49-7699;
142 PHS; 143 above PHS, below left
PD/NIH, below right PHS; 144 left Courtesy of George Moore, above right PHS,
below right Oregon State Board of
Health/PHS; 145 PHS.

Chapter Seven
Page 147 PHS; 148 above NLM, below PHS; 149 NLM; 150 & 151 VIC/NIH; 152 above left PHS, above right PHS, below PHS; 154 & 155 *Medical World News*, January 26, 1968, reprinted by permission; 156 & 157 NLM; 159 CDC; 160 above NLM, below NLM; 161 above NINCDS, below NLM; 162 above PHS/Ben Shahn, photographer, below left PHS, below right PHS; 164 above FDA, below FDA; 166 NLM; 167 PHS; 169 above PHS, below PHS.

Chapter Eight
Page 171 PHS; 172 above Courtesy of Merlin DuVal, below left Courtesy of Paul Ehrlich, below right Courtesy of William Stewart; 173 PHS; 174 NIOSH; 175 NIOSH; 176 & 177 FDA; 178 above left SEHM, above right ADAMHA, below SEHM; 180 & 181 Courtesy of Stuart Mackler; 183 above PHS, below left PHS, below right Portfolio Associates Inc. for the PHS; 184 above CDC, below Portfolio Associates Inc. for the PHS; 185 PHS; 186 above left PHS, above right NHLBI, below PHS; 188 Courtesy of Thomas Monath; 189 Courtesy of Thomas Monath; 190 & 191 Courtesy of James Moore; 193 NIH.

Chapter Nine
Page 195 FDA; 196 OSH/CDC; 197 AP-Wide World Photos; 198 above Gene Basset, Courtesy of the *Atlanta Journal* and United Features, below Courtesy of Pat Crowley, *Palm Beach Post*; 199 above Jimmy Margulies, copyright 1984, reprinted by permission, below Dick Locher, reprinted by permission, Tribune Media Services; 200 above PHS, below NIH; 201 above NCI, below CDC; 202 above left NIDA, above right NIDA, below left NIDA, below right NLM; 205 above CDC, below CDC; 206 NIH; 208 FDA; 209 ATSDR; 210 & 211 PHS.

Surgeons General of The United States Public Health Service

John M. Woodworth
1871-1879 (died)

John B. Hamilton
1879-1891

Walter Wyman
1891-1911 (died)

Rupert Blue
1912-1920

Hugh S. Cumming
1920-1936

Thomas Parran
1936-1948

Leonard A. Scheele
1948-1956

Leroy E. Burney
1956-1961

Luther L. Terry
1961-1965

William H. Stewart
1965-1969

Jesse L. Steinfeld
1969-1973

S. Paul Ehrlich (Acting)
1973-1977

Julius B. Richmond
1977-1981

C. Everett Koop
1981-1989

Assistant Secretaries for Health

Department of Health and Human Services
(Health, Education, and Welfare)

Philip R. Lee
1967-1969

Roger O. Egeberg
1969-1971

Merlin K. DuVal
1971-1972

Charles C. Edwards
1973-1975

Theodore Cooper
1975-1977

Julius B. Richmond
1977-1981

Edward N. Brandt
1981-1984

Robert E. Windom
1986-1989

James O. Mason
1989-

Bibliography

A List of Selected Readings in Public Health Service History.

Brandt, Allan M. *No Magic Bullet: A Social History of Venereal Disease in the United States since 1880.* Expanded ed. New York: Oxford University Press, 1987.

Dworsky, Leonard. *Conservation in the United States: A Documentary History.* New York: Chelsea House, 1971.

Etheridge, Elizabeth W. *The Believers: A History of the Epidemic Intelligence Service of the Centers for Disease Control.* An unpublished manuscript.

————. *The Butterfly Caste: A Social History of Pellagra in the South.* Westport, Connecticut: Greenwood Press, 1972.

Ettling, John. *The Germ of Laziness: Rockefeller Philanthropy and Public Health in the New South.* Cambridge: Harvard University Press, 1981.

Federal Security Agency. Public Health Service. *The United States Cadet Nurse Corps and Other Federal Nurse Training Programs.* Washington, D.C.: GPO, 1950. (PHS Pub. No. 38).

Furman, Bess. *A Profile of the United States Public Health Service, 1798-1948.* Washington, D.C.: U.S. Department of Health, Education and Welfare, 1973. (DHEW Pub. No. [NIH]73-369).

————. n.d. Unpublished manuscript in the collections of the History of Medicine Division, National Library of Medicine, Bethesda, Maryland.

Grubbs, Samuel B. *By Order of the Surgeon General: Thirty-seven Years Active Duty in the Public Health Service.* Greenfield, Indiana: Wm. Mitchell Printing Co., 1943.

Harden, Victoria. *Inventing the NIH: Federal Biomedical Research Policy, 1887-1937.* Baltimore: Johns Hopkins University Press, c1986.

————. *Rocky Mountain Spotted Fever: A Twentieth Century Disease.* Baltimore: Johns Hopkins University Press, forthcoming.

Harris, Ruth Ray. *Dental Services in a New Age: A History of the National Institute of Dental Research.* Rockville, Maryland: Montrose Press, 1989.

Heatherly, Charles L., ed. *Mandate for Leadership: Policy Management in a Conservative Administration.* Washington, D.C.: Heritage Foundation, c1981.

Heiser, Victor. *An American Doctor's Odyssey: Adventures in Forty-five Countries.* New York: W.W. Norton, c1936.

Jones, James H. *Bad Blood: The Tuskegee Syphilis Experiment.* New York: Free Press, c1981.

Miles, Rufus. *The Department of Health, Education, and Welfare.* New York: Praeger, [c1974].

Mountin, Joseph W. *Selected Papers of Joseph W. Mountin, M.D.* n.p.: Joseph W. Mountin Memorial Committee, 1956.

Neustadt, Richard E., and Harvey V. Fineberg. *The Epidemic That Never Was: Policy Making and the Swine Flu Affair.* New York: Vintage Books, 1983, c1982.

Ogden, Horace G. *CDC and the Smallpox Crusade.* Washington, D.C.: U.S. Department of Health and Human Services, Public Health Service, Center for Disease Control, 1987. (HHS Pub. No. (CDC) 87-8400).

Redman, Eric. *The Dance of Legislation.* New York: Simon and Schuster, c1973.

Rosen, George. *A History of Public Health.* New York: MD Publications, [c1958].

Sardell, Alice. *The U.S. Experiment in Social Medicine: The Community Health Center Program, 1965-1986.* Pittsburgh, Pennsylvania: University of Pittsburgh Press, c1988.

Schmeckebier, Laurence F. *The Public Health Service: Its History, Activities and Organization.* Baltimore: Johns Hopkins Press, 1923.

Shorter, Edward. *The Health Century.* New York: Doubleday, 1987.

Sidel, Victor W. and Ruth Sidel, eds. *Reforming Medicine: Lessons of the Last Quarter Century.* New York: Pantheon, c1984.

Silverstein, Arthur M. *Pure Politics and Impure Science: The Swine Flu Affair.* Baltimore: Johns Hopkins University Press, c1981.

Smillie, Wilson G. *Public Health: Its Promise for the Future.* New York: Macmillan, 1955.

Starr, Paul. *The Social Transformation of American Medicine.* New York: Basic Books, c1982.

Straus, Robert. *Medical Care for Seamen: The Origin of Public Medical Service in the United States.* New Haven: Yale University Press, 1950.

Strickland, Stephen Parks. *Politics, Science and Dread Disease: A Short History of the United States Medical Research Policy.* Cambridge: Harvard University Press, 1972.

Thurm, Richard H., *For the Relief of the Sick and Disabled: The U.S. Public Health Service Hospital at Boston, 1799-1969.* Washington, D.C.: GPO, 1972. (1729-0010).

Tobey, James A. *The National Government and Public Health.* Baltimore: Johns Hopkins Press, 1926.

Trask, John W. *The United States Marine Hospital, Port of Boston: An Account of Its Origin and Briefly of Its History and of the Physicians Who Have Been in Charge.* [Washington, D.C.]: Federal Security Agency, U.S. Public Health Service, 1940.

U.S. Department of Health and Human Services. *Reducing the Health Consequences of Smoking: 25 Years of Progress. A Report of the Surgeon General.* U.S. Department of Health and Human Services, Public Health Service, Centers for Disease Control, Center for Chronic Disease Prevention and Health Promotion, Office on Smoking and Health. (DHHS Pub. No. (CDC) 89-8411). Pre-publication version, January 11, 1989.

U.S. Department of Health and Human Services. Bureau of Health Professions. *Supply of Manpower in Selected Health Occupations: 1950-1990.* (DHHS Pub. No. (HRA) 80-35).

U.S. Marine Hospital Service. *Annual Report.* 1st-30th; 1871/72-1900/01.

U.S. Office of the Assistant Secretary for Health and Surgeon General. *Healthy People: The Surgeon General's Report on Health Promotion and Disease Prevention.* Washington, D.C.: GPO, 1979. (DHEW (PHS) Pub. No. 79-55071).

U.S. Public Health and Marine Hospital Service. *Annual Report of the Surgeon General.* 1901/02-1910/11.

U.S. Public Health Service. *Annual Report to the Congress.* 1973/74————.

U.S. Public Health Service. Office of the Assistant Secretary for Health. Office of Organization and Management Systems. *Historical Profile of the Leadership of the Public Health Service, 1944-1988.* [Rockville, Maryland?]: The Service, 1988.

United States Public Health Service. Study Group on Mission and Organization of the Public Health Service. *Final Report.* [Washington, D.C.: GPO, 1960].

U.S. Surgeon General's Advisory Committee on Smoking and Health. *Smoking and Health: Report of the Advisory Committee to the Surgeon General of the Public Health Service.* Washington, D.C.: GPO, [1964]. (PHS Pub. No. 1103).

Williams, Ralph C. *The United States Public Health Service, 1798-1950.* Washington, D.C.: Commissioned Officers Association of the United States Public Health Service, [1951].

Index

A

Abdellah, Faye, 201
Act of 1902, 48
Adams, John, 14
Addiction, 85
Agriculture, Department of, 56, 63
AIDS, 194, 197, 199, 202-9, 211
Alcoholism, 85, 177, 201
American Academy of Arts and
    Sciences, 17
American Association for the
    Advancement of Science, 55-56
American Cancer Society (ACS), 149
American Heart Association (AHA),
    149
American Medical Association
    (AMA), 58, 95, 109, 133; and
    the National Tuberculosis
    Association, 134; and "state
    medicine," 131
American Public Health Association,
    22, 25, 53
Anfinsen, Christian, 165
Annual Report, 29, 48, 53; on the care
    of veterans, 75, 80; on the Office
    of Statistical Investigations, 85
Antibiotics, 65, 86
Appropriations Act (1913), 68
Army, U.S., 25, 72, 74, 115, 116
Arnstein, Margaret, 162
AZT, 211

B

Bacteriology, 32, 35, 82
Baehr, George, 115
Bauer, Gary, 204
Bayfield (hospital ship), 116
Bear (Coast Guard cutter), 118
Bennett, William, 204
Billings, John Shaw, 19, 20, 22, 25;
    and the National Library of
    Medicine, 136
Biologics Control Act (1902), 39
Biostatistics, 85
Blindness, 42, 65, 67
Blue, Rupert, 58, 68, 80, 82
Boston Marine Hospital, 19
Boutwell, George S., 19, 20
Brandt, Edward, 194, 203, 207
Branham, John, 53
Braund, Ralph, 116
British Navy, 14
Broder, Samuel, 204
Bulletin, 26
Bureau of Indian Affairs (BIA), 134,
    139
Bureau of Mines, 56
Burke, Thomas, 207
Burney, Leroy, 100, 138, 141-45; and
    radiation related PHS activities,
    142; replacement of, 146; on
    smoking, 148, 149
Bush, George, 200

C

Cadet Nurse Corps, 120, 122, 126
Califano, Joseph, 185, 191
Carr, Ralph, 132
Carter, Henry Rose, 61, 63
Carter, Jimmy, 185, 187
Celebrezze, Anthony, 154
Centers for Disease Control (CDC),
    125, 162, 177, 192, 203, 207; and
    EIS, 139, 141; and fever
    epidemics, 189, 204; and
    smallpox, 165; and venereal
    disease, 182
Cerebro-spinal fever, 29
Child Hygiene Investigations, 112
Children's Bureau, 56, 95, 104, 166; and
    a "National Health Plan," 109
Cholera, 32, 39, 42, 48
Civilian Conservation Corps, 102,
    104, 110
Civil Service, 40
Civil Service Act, 22
Civil War, 19, 156
Cleveland, Grover, 31, 53
Coast Guard, 28, 118, 119
Cohen, Wilbur, 158, 168
Comanche (Coast Guard cutter), 115
Commissioned Corps, 122, 145, 154,
    162, 173, 185, 203, 207
Committee of One Hundred for
    National Health, 55
Congress, 39, 53, 153, 165; and
    environmental health, 142; and
    the establishment of a Narcotics
    Division, 85; Fifth (1798), 14;
    First (1788), 14; and HEW, 133,
    153; and the Hospital Survey and
    Construction Act (1946), 125-26;
    and smoking, 149-50
Conjunctivitis, 45
Cooper, Theodore, 179
Cumming, Hugh S., 82, 86, 90, 104;
    and the AMA, 110; and
    Lumsden, rivalry between, 95,
    99; and the Pan American